MW00823962

Learning Objectives

The goals of Chapter 2 are to help readers do the follow.

1. Recognize where critical decisions are made in research projects using text corpora.

2. Be familiar with research designs for text-based projects that operate at different levels of analysis.

R esearch design is one of the most critically important but also most difficult topics in social science (Creswell, 2014; Gorard, 2013). Research design is essentially concerned with the basic architecture of research projects, with designing projects as systems that allow theory, data, and method to interface in such a way as to maximize a project's ability to achieve its goals (Becker & Denicolo, 2012). Research design involves a sequence of decisions that have to be taken in a project's early stages, when one oversight or poor decision can lead to results that are ultimately trivial or untrustworthy. Thus, it is critically important to think carefully and systematically about research design before committing time and resources to acquiring texts or mastering software packages or programming languages for text mining and analysis.

We begin this chapter with a review of the major principles of social science research design that are applicable to text mining and text analysis projects. We discuss the differences between research performed at different *levels of analysis*, different strategies for *case selection* and *text sampling*, and several forms of *inferential logic* that are commonly used in text-based research. We then review six of the most prominent approaches to social science text analysis (*analysis of discourse positions, conversation analysis, critical discourse analysis, content analysis, Foucauldian intertextuality*, and *analysis of texts as social information*), analyzing in detail the research design used in several recently published examples of each type of research.

Levels of Analysis

While text mining and text analysis methods can be challenging to use in even basic applications, theoretically oriented social science research projects place additional demands on the use of these methods. These demands derive in part from the multiple levels of analysis that are endemic to social research. Ruiz Ruiz (2009) usefully proposed three main levels of analysis at which social science text analysis research can potentially operate: the level of *the text itself*, the level of the immediate social and intertextual *context*, and a *sociological* level that involves attempts to identify causal relations between texts and the social and societal contexts in which they are produced and received. Approaches to text analysis research developed within various academic disciplines generally operate at one or another of these levels, and awareness of these levels allows us to more readily comprehend differences and similarities between the research designs used within these different approaches.

The Textual Level

Social science text analysis at the textual level "involves characterizing or determining the composition and structure" of a discourse (Ruiz Ruiz, 2009). Most of the methods introduced in Parts III and IV of this book are concerned with analyzing texts at the textual level in terms of their topics and themes (Chapter 7), narrative structures (Chapter 8), metaphors (Chapter 9), and other aspects of the composition and structure of texts themselves.

The Contextual Level

In addition to revealing patterns in texts themselves, text analysis can also reveal elements of the social context in which texts are produced and received, including situational contexts in which the text has been produced and characteristics of the texts' authors. As we will see, social scientists have developed several methods of situational text analysis, including analysis of discourse positions and conversation analysis. The context of discourse is not only situational but also intertextual, as all texts exist in a symbolic universe, made up partly of other texts, in which they acquire meaning. Foucauldian intertextuality permits researchers to analyze texts by referring to the discourses that circulate in the social space in which the text is produced and received.

The Sociological Level

Analyzing texts at a sociological level involves making connections between the texts analyzed and the social spaces in which they are produced and received. Texts can be analyzed sociologically only if they are first analyzed at both textual and contextual levels. While connections between texts and their social spaces can vary depending on the analyst's research questions and theoretical orientation, they can be roughly sorted in terms of two categories: research that analyzes texts as reflections of the *ideology* of their authors and audience and research that analyzes texts as *social information*.

Strategies for Document Selection and Sampling

While Chapter 3 provides technical instruction regarding using web scraping and web crawling methods to collect textual data, in this section we focus on strategic aspects of case selection and data sampling as they relate to corpus-based research design. Text selection and sampling strategies are critically related to a project's research question (when there is a well-formulated question); the availability and accessibility of texts; the specific tools, including software packages and programming languages, that are used to collect textual data; and the form of inferential logic used in the analysis.

Case Selection

Data selection and data sampling are of central importance in connecting theory and data in any empirical research project. While the term *case selection* is used mainly in qualitative and mixed methods research projects where the generalizability of the findings from such projects can be increased by the strategic selection of small numbers of cases to analyze, in this section we borrow the language of case selection from qualitative and mixed methods research to discuss how social scientists can most strategically select sources of textual data for different types of research projects.

Corpus-based social science research always involves data selection, and the more strategically documents are selected, the more likely it is that a research project will achieve its goals. When the objective of a project is to achieve the greatest possible amount of information about a phenomenon, selecting a *representative case* (data that are representative of a larger population) or a *random sample* (see later in this chapter) may not be the optimal strategy because the typical or average case is often not the richest in information. Atypical or *extreme cases* often reveal more information because they activate more actors and more basic mechanisms in the situation studied. The extreme case can be well suited for getting a point across in an especially dramatic way, which often occurs for well-known social science case studies such as Freud's "Wolf Man" (Freud, 1918/2011) or Foucault's (1975) "Panopticon." Examples of the use of extreme cases in text analysis research include a 2004 study of boys engaging in "slut bashing" by Bamberg (see Chapter 8) and a 2003 study of animal and death metaphors in high-technology jargon by Ignatow (see Chapter 9). The texts analyzed in these studies are not necessarily statistically representative of the social groups that produce them, and the groups themselves are not representative of the general population. Instead, the texts analyzed were selected because their language was seen as extreme or unusual in a way that appeared relevant to theoretical debates.

A *critical case* can be defined as having strategic importance in relation to the general problem.

For example, an occupational medicine clinic wanted to investigate whether people working with organic solvents suffered brain damage. Instead of choosing a representative sample among all those enterprises in the clinic's area that used organic solvents, the clinic strategically located a single workplace where all safety regulations on cleanliness, air quality, and the like, had been fulfilled. This model enterprise became a critical case: if brain damage related to organic solvents could be found at this particular facility, then it was likely that the same problem would exist at other enterprises which were less careful with safety regulations for organic solvents. (Flyvbjerg, 2001)

Selecting critical cases allows social scientists to save time and money in studying a given phenomenon by formulating a generalization of the form "'If it is valid for this case, it is valid for all (or many) cases.' In its negative form, the generalization would be, 'If it is not valid for this case, then it is not valid for any (or only few) cases'" (Denzin & Lincoln, 2011, p. 307). An example of the use of critical cases in text analysis research is Gibson and Zellmer-Bruhn's 2001 mixed method metaphor analysis of employee attitudes in four countries (see Chapter 9). The four countries were strategically selected for comparison in order to maximize geographical and cultural variation so that the findings could be generalized.

Text Sampling

In practice, many text analysis projects do not begin with a clearly formulated research question but rather with a collection of documents. Researchers often come across interesting or unique document collections that they want to use for research projects, and they may not be concerned with "the potential problem of having to undo or compensate for the biases in such data" (Krippendorff, 2013, p. 122). The technical term for this approach to data acquisition is *convenience sampling*. In convenience sampling, the data selection strategies discussed later in this chapter are not applicable, as the researcher will use inductive or abductive rather than deductive logic to make inferences from the data. Conversely, researchers whose projects start with a research question, whether it is mainly theoretical or substantive, must carefully consider data selection strategies in order to set up a research design that can potentially answer the research question or questions before moving on to choosing a data sampling strategy.

Once a researcher has identified documents to be analyzed, it may be necessary to implement a sampling strategy. Unless the researcher can acquire and analyze all the data from a given source (e.g., every article in a newspaper archive or every comment from a social media site), a sampling strategy of one kind or another will be needed. Although in the early 2000s a small number of big data advocates claimed that big data's sheer size would obviate the need for statistical sampling (see Chapter 1), for social scientists to take maximum advantages of the variety and volume of online archives, sampling is as critical than ever (see Schradie, 2013).

Sampling is often performed for the purpose of creating *representative samples,* which are samples that are statistically representative of the broader population from which they are drawn. Representative sampling allows findings to be generalized from the sample to the larger population. The ideal representative sample is a *probability sample,* which allows researchers to generalize their findings to the larger population through statistical inferences. However, in corpus-based research there are significant barriers to obtaining representative probability samples. Krippendorff (2013) went so far as to argue that the challenge faced by text analysts of sampling from one population in view of another "differs radically from the problems addressed by statistical sampling theory" (p. 114). For example, a social scientist can sample users' comments on a social media platform such as Facebook or Twitter, but it is almost impossible to sample in such a way as to be able to generalize from the sample to the entire universe of Facebook or Twitter users. There are also some fundamental differences between textual data and the sort of individual-level data that is typically used in large-scale social research projects such as social surveys. Where for social surveys the unit of analysis is the indivisible, independent individual, for texts the unit of analysis can be conceived in many ways, including the following:

> . . . in terms of hierarchies in which one level includes the next (film genre, movie, scene, episode, encounter, shot, assertion/action, frame, and so on . . .). They could be read as sequentially ordered events, jointly constituting narratives whose integrity would be lost if the components were permuted, or as networks of intertextualities (co-occurring, making reference to, building on, or erasing each other). There is no single "natural" way of counting texts. (Krippendorff, 2013, p. 113)

In addition, in corpus-based research the units sampled are rarely the units counted. For example a researcher may sample newspaper articles from an archive but count words or word co-occurrences (rather than articles). Even when researchers do settle on units of analysis for sampling and counting and adopt probability sampling techniques, biases can occur. Certain groups may be systematically excluded from data collection or may be underrepresented due to self-selection biases. Collecting representative samples using the Internet has thus been considered highly problematic for some time (Hewson & Laurent, 2012).

Representative probability samples are rare in corpus-based research, but social scientists have other sampling strategies available to them. A first element in any sampling strategy is *enumeration,* or assigning numbers to or comprehensively listing the units within a population. Some digital archives have documents that are already enumerated, but it is often left to the researcher to arrange units into ordered lists that can be enumerated.

Once the researcher has an enumerated population of units, they may sample from the population using *random sampling* by employing a randomization device such as software or an online random number generator. Alternatively, or sometimes in addition, they may use *systematic sampling* where they sample every *kth* unit from an enumerated list. However, as the interval *k* is a constant, systematic sampling may create a rhythm to the sampling that leads to bias. For example, by sampling YouTube user comments starting on a Saturday and then every seven days, a researcher would risk biasing the sample toward comments about videos that are more popular on weekends, which may differ systematically from videos that are watched on weekdays.

Researchers can also use *stratified sampling,* which involves sampling from within subunits, or strata, of a population. For instance, a researcher interested in readers' comments on newspaper articles could create a stratified sample from the most popular newspaper sections (e.g., world news, business, arts and entertainment, sports) and then randomly or systematically sample from each of these strata. Of course the selection of strata would depend on the research question or questions guiding the project. Researchers can also use *varying probability sampling* to sample proportionately from data sources with different sizes or levels of importance, such as newspapers with different circulation levels (Krippendorff, 2013, p. 117).

A widely used sampling technique in qualitative research is *snowball sampling,* which is an iterative procedure in which a researcher starts with a small sample and then repeatedly applies a sampling criterion until a sample size limit is reached. For instance, a social scientist could record and transcribe interviews with each of the members of a close-knit group, then request that each member provide contact information for three friends and interview each of these, and then repeat the process with each friend until the sample size limit is reached and the researcher has acquired enough data to begin analysis. *Relevance sampling,* or *purposive sampling,* is a more research question–driven, nonprobabilistic sampling technique in which the researcher learns about a population of interest and then gradually reduces the number of texts to be analyzed based on the texts' relevance to the research question. For corpus-based social science research, relevance sampling is "so natural that it is rarely discussed as a category of its own" (Krippendorff 2013, p. 121). As a social scientist designs a project, it is only natural that they would eliminate data that is not directly relevant to their research questions. For instance, a social scientist interested in women's groups or pages on Facebook could purposively sample women's groups and eliminate groups and pages that focus on men's issues or issues not directly related to women. Such purposive sampling restricts the representativeness of the sample and the generalizability of the results, but in many projects these will be secondary concerns.

Types of Inferential Logic

Inferential logic lies at the heart of social science research. Based on their analysis of collected data, social scientists use specific forms of logic to make inferences about relationships among empirical phenomena and between empirical phenomena and theoretical propositions and generalizations. In the early stages of a project, a researcher may not know the sorts of inferences they will make or conclusions they will draw, but by the project's end, they will inevitably have used one or more of the following forms of inferential logic. As we will see, different approaches to text mining and text analysis differ systematically in their use of inferential logic.

Inductive Logic

Inductive logic involves making inferences by working upward from empirical data to theoretical generalizations and propositions. Researchers begin by analyzing empirical data with their preferred tools, and then allow general conclusions to emerge organically from their analysis. When ethnographic researchers use inductive logic, they often position their research as *grounded theory* (Glaser & Strauss, 1967), while more quantitatively oriented researchers refer to *data mining*.

The use of inductive inference is attractive to social scientists for several reasons. It allows them to work with data sets and specialized tools quickly without having to invest time mastering abstruse theories or setting up complex research designs. It also allows for great flexibility and adaptability, as analysts can allow their data to speak to them and can adjust their conclusions accordingly rather than imposing their preferred categories and concepts onto their data in an artificial manner. And inductive research designs allow quantitatively oriented researchers in particular to immediately make use of very large corpora and powerful software and programming languages. But as we will discuss briefly in Chapter 7, in its purest forms, induction has serious drawbacks. It encourages social scientists to begin research projects without first formulating research questions on the assumption that the project's purpose will become evident during its analysis phase. There is a very real risk that this simply will not happen, and the researcher will have invested significant time and resources in a project that is directionless and ultimately purposeless. Purely inductive research can also encourage researcher passivity with regard to mastering the literatures in their areas of interest. Rather than mastering the work that has been done by others so as to identify gaps in knowledge, unsolved puzzles, or critical disagreements and then designing a study to address one or a few of these, induction encourages researchers to skip straight to data collection and analysis and then work backward from their findings to the pertinent gaps in the literature, puzzles, and disagreements. In practice, this is often a high-risk strategy.

Although the exclusive use of inductive inferential logic has its drawbacks, induction is and should be an element in virtually all social science research. The complexity of natural language data in particular demands of researchers that they allow their data to alter their theoretical models and frameworks rather than force data to conform to their preferred theories.

An example of a research design based on inductive logic is Frith and Gleeson's 2004 thematic analysis of male undergraduate students' responses to open-ended survey items related to clothing and body image. The undergraduates were recruited through snowball sampling. In order to better understand how men's feelings about their bodies influence their clothing practices, Frith and Gleeson (2004) analyzed written answers to four questions about clothing practices and body image and discovered four main themes relevant to their research question, including *men value practicality, men should not care how they look, clothes are used to conceal or reveal*, and *clothes are used to fit a cultural ideal*. Another example of inductive text analysis is Jones, Coviello, and Tang's (2011) study of academic research on the academic field of international entrepreneurship research. Jones and colleagues (2011) constructed a corpus from 323 journal articles on international entrepreneurship published between 1989 and 2009 and inductively synthesized and categorized themes and subthemes in their data (see Chapter 7).

Deductive Logic

Deductive logic is the form of inferential logic most closely associated with the traditional scientific method applied to deterministic (or pseudodeterministic) phenomena (cf. Macy & Willer, 2002). Deductive research designs start with theoretical abstractions, derive hypotheses from these abstractions, and then set up research projects that test these hypotheses on empirical data. The purest form of such a research design is the laboratory experiment, which allows social scientists to control all variables except for those of theoretical interest and then determine unequivocally whether hypotheses derived from a theory are supported or not.

While big data and powerful software and programming languages allow researchers to rely on inductive reasoning in many research designs, in our view, theory, hypothesis testing, and deductive reasoning are as central to social science research today as they ever have been. Deductive inferential logic has been applied in many corpus-based studies. An early example is Hirschman's (1987) study "People as Products," which tested an established theory of resource exchange on male- and female-placed personal advertisements. In total, Hirschman derived 16 hypotheses from this theory and tested these hypotheses on a year's series of personal dating advertisements collected from *New York Magazine* and *Washingtonian* magazine. Hirschman selected at random 100 male-placed and 100 female-placed advertisements, as well as 20 additional advertisements that she used to establish content categories for the analysis. One male and one female coder coded the advertisements in terms of the categories derived from the 20 additional advertisements. The data were transformed to represent the proportionate weight of each resource category coded (e.g., money, physical status, occupational status) for each sample, and the data were analyzed with a 2x2 analysis of variance (ANOVA) procedure in which gender of advertiser (male or female) and city (New York or Washington) served as factors.

Management researchers Gibson and Zellmer-Bruhn's 2001 study of concepts of teamwork across national organizational cultures is another example of the use of deductive inferential logic in a corpus-based project. This study's goal was to test an established theory of the influence of national culture on employees' attitudes. Gibson and Zellmer-Bruhn (2001) tested this theory on data from four organizations in four different countries (France, the Philippines, Puerto Rico, and the United States), conducting interviews that they transcribed to form their corpora. They used QSR NUD*IST (which subsequently evolved into NVivo) and TACT (Popping, 1997) to organize qualitative coding of five frequently used teamwork metaphors, which were then used to create dependent variables for hypothesis testing using multinomial logit and logistic regression (see Chapter 9 for details).

Cunningham, Sagas, Sartore, Amsden, and Schellhase's (2004) analysis of coverage of women's and men's sports in the newsletter *NCAA* (National Collegiate Athletic Association) *News* is another example of a deductive research design. Cunningham and his colleagues tested theories of organizational resource dependence on data from 24 randomly selected issues of the *NCAA News*. One issue of the magazine was selected from each month of the year from the years 1999 and 2001 (systematic sampling). From these issues, the authors chose to analyze only articles specifically focused on athletics, coaches, or their teams, excluding articles focused on committees, facilities, and other topics (*relevance sampling*). Two researchers independently coded each of 5,745 paragraphs in the sample for gender (male, female, or combined) and for the paragraph's location within the magazine (front page, back page, top of page, or other) and content. Reliability coefficients including Cohen's kappa and the Pearson product-moment coefficient were calculated, as were frequency distributions, chi-square statistics, and ANOVA.

There are significant challenges involved in using the hypothetico-deductive model of research with advanced text mining and text analysis tools (see Parts II–IV). As these tools produce sophisticated outputs such as semantic network graphs and co-occurrence matrices rather than simple frequency counts, it becomes challenging to formulate hypotheses that can potentially be supported or disconfirmed. Thus, many of the more sophisticated tools that have been developed have been used in projects that either demonstrate these tools' technical advantages relative to lower-tech methods, or for exploratory analysis. As social scientists use increasingly sophisticated text mining and text analysis methods, we anticipate that they will find new ways to integrate these methods into deductive research designs. Still, the extreme complexity of user-generated texts poses challenges for the scientific method. One cannot perform laboratory experiments on the texts that result from interactions among members of large online communities. And even social researchers who are familiar with the relevant literatures in their field may not know precisely what they want to look for when they begin their analysis. For these and other reasons, many social scientists who work with text corpora and text analysis methodologies advocate for abductive inferential logic, a more forensic logic that is commonly used in social science but also in natural science fields such as geology and astronomy, where experiments are rarely performed.

Abductive Logic

Induction and deduction say nothing about how theories are discovered in the first place. The inferential logic that is intended to account for scientific innovation is *abduction,* also known (approximately) as "inference to the best explanation" (see Lipton, 2003). Abduction differs from induction and deduction in that abduction involves an inference in which the conclusion is a hypothesis that can then be tested with a modified or new research design. The term *abduction* was originally defined by the philosopher Charles Sanders Peirce, who held the following:

> Accepting the conclusion that an explanation is needed when facts contrary to what we should expect emerge, it follows that the explanation must be such a proposition as would lead to the prediction of the observed facts, either as necessary conse-quences or at least as very probable under the circumstances. A hypothesis, then, has to be adopted, which is likely in itself, and renders the facts likely. This step of adopting a hypothesis as being suggested by the facts, is what I call abduction. (Peirce, 1901, pp. 202–203)

Abduction "seeks no algorithm, but is a heuristic for luckily finding new things and creating insights" (Bauer, Bicquelet, & Suerdem, 2014). Abductive logic does not replace deduction and induction but *iteratively* bridges them, resembling the reasoning of detec-tives who interpret clues that permit a course of events to be reconstructed or of doctors when making inferences about the presence of illness based on patients' symptoms.

Bauer and colleagues (2014) and Ruiz Ruiz (2009) have advocated for abduction as an appropriate inferential logic for corpus-based research. Bauer, Suerdem, and Bicquelet argued that with abduction, text analysis need not do the following:

> . . . face a dilemma between the Scylla of deduction on the one hand, and Charybdis of induction on the other. We suggest abductive logic as the middle way out of this forced choice: the logic of inference to the most plausible explanation of the given evidence, considering less plausible alternatives. As it entails both machine inference and human intuition, it can maintain the human-machine-text trialogue. (Bauer et al., 2014)

The main problem of abductive inference lies in how to formulate an abduction. Peirce (1901) was not especially clear on this point when he referred to a "flash of understanding" or when attributing abductive capacity to an adaptive human need to explain surprising or unexpected facts. Peirce (1901) did propose criteria to dis-tinguish between good and bad abduction, which include the need for abduction to propose truly new ideas or explanations, the need to derive empirically contrastable predictions from the hypotheses, and the need for the hypotheses to fit in with or give an adequate account of the social and historical context in which they emerge.

Abductive inferential logic is compatible with the use of any number of sophisti-cated research tools and is used in the early stages of many deductive research designs. One example is Ruiz Ruiz's (2009) text analysis of transcriptions of discussions with Spanish manual workers. In the transcripts, the workers are seen as criticizing the chauvinism and submissiveness of Moorish immigrants from Morocco. Ruiz Ruiz described his use of abductive logic but also of inductive and deductive logics, of inference in his 2009 survey of discourse analysis methods.

Approaches to Research Design

Having reviewed a number of foundational concepts in corpus-based social science research design, in this section we review six of the most prominent approaches to social science text analysis, including analysis of discourse positions, conversation analysis, critical discourse analysis, content analysis, Foucauldian intertextuality, and analysis of texts as social information. These approaches are each based on different theoretical foundations and epistemological and ontological positions (see Chapter 1). They also operate at different levels of analysis (see earlier in this chapter) and employ different document selection and sampling strategies and different forms of inferential logic. We analyze in detail the research design used in recently published examples of each approach.

Analysis of Discourse Positions

Discourse positions are understood as typical discursive roles that people adopt in their everyday communication practices, and the analysis of discourse positions is a way of linking texts to the social spaces in which they have emerged. Analysis of discourse positions allows researchers to reconstruct communicative interactions through which texts are produced and in this way gain a better understanding of their meaning from their author's viewpoint. Examples of contemporary discourse position research include studies by Bamberg of the "small stories" told by adolescents and post-adolescents about their identities (Bamberg, 2004) and Edley and Wetherell's (1997; Wetherell & Edley, 1999) studies of masculine identity formation.

Bamberg's 2004 study is informed by theories of human development and of narrative (see Chapter 8), although it does not feature a deductive research design. Like most studies of discourse positions, his study operates at a contextual level of analysis. His texts are excerpts of transcriptions from a group discussion between five 15-year-old boys who engage in slut bashing while telling a story about a female student. The group discussion was conducted in the presence of an adult moderator, but the data were collected as part of a larger project in which Bamberg and his colleagues collected journal entries and transcribed oral accounts from 10-, 12-, and 15-year-old boys in different discursive contexts, including one-on-one interviews, group discussions, and peer interactions. Although the interviews and group discussions were open-ended, they all focused on the same list of topics, including friends and friendships, girls, the boys' feelings and sense of self, and their ideas about adulthood and future orientation. Bamberg and his team analyzed the transcripts line by line, coding instances of the boys' positioning themselves relative to each other and to characters in their stories.

Conversation Analysis

Conversation analysis studies everyday conversations in terms of how people negotiate the meaning of the conversation in which they are participating and of the larger discourse of which the conversation is a part. Conversation analysts focus not only on what is said in daily conversations but on how people use language pragmatically to define the situations in which they find themselves—a process that goes mostly unnoticed until there is disagreement as to the meaning of a particular situation. Recent examples of conversation analysis include studies of conversation in educational settings by O'Keefe and Walsh (2012) and Evison (2013); in health care settings by Heath and Luff (2000), Heritage and Raymond (2005), and Silverman (1997); and online among Wikipedia editors by Danescu-Niculescu-Mizil, Lee, Pang, and Kleinberg (2012).

In her 2013 study of "academic talk," the educational researcher Jane Evison used corpus linguistic techniques on both a corpus of 250,000 words of spoken academic discourse and a benchmark corpus of casual conversation to explore conversational turn openings. The corpus of academic discourse included 13,337 turns taken by tutors and students in a range of pedagogical encounters. In seeking to better understand the unique language of academia and of specific disciplines, Evison identified six items that have a particularly strong affinity with the turn-opening position (*mhm, mm, yes, laughter, oh, no*) as key characteristics of academic talk.

Roya Hakimnia and her colleagues' conversation analysis of transcripts of calls to a telenursing site in Sweden used a comparative research design (Hakimnia, Holmström, Carlsson, & Höglund, 2014). The study's goal was to analyze callers' reasons for calling and the outcomes of the calls in terms of whether men and women received different kinds of referrals. The researchers chose to randomly sample 800 calls from a corpus of over 5,000 total calls. The calls had been recorded at a telenursing site in Sweden over a period of 11 months. Callers were informed about the study in a prerecorded message and consented to participate by entering a certain number on the telephone, while the nurses were informed verbally about the study. The first step in the analysis of the sample of 800 calls was to create a matrix including information on each caller's gender, age, fluency or nonfluency in Swedish, and the outcome of the call (whether callers were referred to a general practitioner). The data in the matrix was analyzed in SPSS 19 using chi-square tests for categorical data and odds ratios for the outcomes of calls.

Critical Discourse Analysis

Pioneered by Fairclough (1995), critical discourse analysis involves seeking the presence of features from other discourses in the text or discourse to be analyzed. Fairclough's concept of intertextuality is based on the idea that people appropriate from discourses circulating in their social space whenever they speak or write. Ordinary activities involving speaking and writing are thus understood to be equivalent to selecting and combining elements from dominant discourses.

While the term *discourse* is generally used to refer to all practices of writing and talking, for critical discourse analysis, discourses are understood as ways of writing and talking that "rule out" and "rule in" ways of constructing knowledge about topics. In other words, discourses "do not just describe things; they do things" (Potter & Wetherell, 1987, p. 6) through the way they make sense of the world for its inhabitants (Fairclough, 1992; van Dijk, 1993).

Discourses cannot be studied directly; they can only be explored by examining the texts that constitute them (Fairclough, 1992; Parker, 1992). In this way, texts can be analyzed as fragments of discourses that reflect and project ideological domination. But texts can also be considered a potential mechanism of liberation when they are produced by the critical analyst who reveals mechanisms of ideological domination in texts in an attempt to overcome or eliminate them.

Although critical discourse analysis has generally employed strictly interpretive methods, use of techniques associated with corpus linguistics is not a novel practice (Krishnamurthy, 1996; Stubbs, 1994), and the use of software to create, manage, and analyze large corpora appears to be increasingly popular (Baker et al., 2008; Koller & Mautner, 2004; O'Halloran & Coffin, 2004). For example, Bednarek and Caple (2014) introduced the concept of "news values" to critical discourse analysis of news media and illustrated their approach with two case studies using the same corpus of British news discourse. Their corpus comprised 100 news stories (about 70,000 words total) from 2003 covering 10 topics from 10 different national newspapers, including 5 quality papers and 5 tabloids. Bednarek and Caple's (2014) analysis proceeded through analysis of word frequency of the top 100 most frequently used words and two-word clusters (bigrams), focusing on words that represent news values such as *eliteness, superlativeness, proximity, negativity, timeliness, personalization,* and *novelty.* The authors concluded that their case studies demonstrated that corpus linguistic techniques can identify discursive devices that are repeatedly used in news discourse to construct and perpetuate an ideology of newsworthiness.

Baker and his colleagues (2008) at Lancaster University have demonstrated that methods normally associated with corpus linguistics can be effectively used for critical discourse analysis. In their research based on the analysis of a 140-million-word corpus of British news articles about refugees, asylum seekers, immigrants, and migrants they discussed how they used collocation and concordance analysis to identify common categories of representation of refugees, asylum seekers, immigrants, and migrants and also how collocation and concordance analysis can be used as well to direct researchers to representative texts in order to carry out qualitative analysis.

Content Analysis

Content analysis adopts a positivist approach to text analysis and is generally focused on texts themselves rather than texts' relations to their social and historical contexts. Although we define the term rather loosely here and in Chapter 7, one of the classic definitions of *content analysis* defines it as "a research technique for the objective, systematic-quantitative description of the manifest content of communication" (Berelson, 1952, p. 18). At a practical level, content analysis involves the development of analytical categories that are used to construct a coding frame that is then applied to textual data. It mainly consists of breaking down texts into pertinent units of information in order to permit subsequent coding and categorization.

Roberts (1997) categorized text analysis techniques in the social sciences as either *thematic*, *network*, or *semantic* techniques. In line with Berelson's (1952) quote (see the previous paragraph), thematic analysis focuses on manifest meanings in texts and includes methods commonly used in business as well as social science, such as topic modeling (see Chapter 15). Network analysis models statistical associations between words to infer the existence of mental models shared by members of a community (see Chapter 7). Semantic analysis, sometimes referred to as *hermeneutic* or *hermeneutic structuralist* techniques, include a variety of methods designed to recognize latent meanings in texts. In Chapters 7, 10, and 13, we cover several thematic, network, and semantic content analysis techniques in detail.

Foucauldian Intertextuality

Michel Foucault's (1973) influential conceptualization of intertextuality differs from Fairclough's conceptualization in critical discourse analysis in that rather than identifying the influence of external discourses within a text, for Foucault the meaning of a text emerges in reference to discourses with which it engages in dialogue, be it explicitly or, more often, implicitly. In Foucauldian intertextual analysis, the analyst must ask each text about its presuppositions and with which discourses it dialogues. The meaning of a text therefore derives from its similarities and differences with respect to other texts and discourses and from implicit presuppositions within the text that can be recognized by historically informed close reading.

Foucauldian intertextual analysis is performed in many fields, not only in fields thought of as highly theoretical or speculative but in applied research fields as well. For instance, in the field of forestry research, a number of studies have used Foucauldian intertextual analysis to analyze forestry policy (see Winkel, 2012, for an overview). Researchers from universities in Europe (e.g., Berglund, 2001; Franklin, 2002; Van Herzele, 2006) and North America but especially from universities in developing countries (e.g., Asher & Ojeda, 2009; Mathews, 2005) have used Foucauldian analysis to study policy discourses regarding forest management, forest fires, and corporate responsibility.

Another recent example of Foucauldian intertextual analysis is a sophisticated study of the professional identities of nurses by Bell, Campbell, and Goldberg (2015). While this study is largely inductive, Bell and colleagues (2015) drew on Foucault's concept of intertextuality in arguing that nurses' professional identities should be understood in relation to the identities of other occupational categories in the health care field. The authors collected their data from PubMed, a medical research database. Using PubMed's own user interface, the authors acquired the abstracts for research papers that used the terms *service* or *services* in the abstract or key words for a period beginning in 1986 and ending in 2013. The downloaded abstracts were added to an SQLite database, which was used to generate comma-separated values (CSV) files with abstracts organized into three-year periods. The authors then spent approximately six weeks of full-time work manually checking the data for duplicates and other errors. The final sample included over 230,000 abstracts. Bell and colleagues (2015) then used the text analysis package Leximancer to calculate frequency and co-occurrence statistics for all concepts in the abstracts. Leximancer also produced concept maps (see Chapter 7) to visually represent the relationships between concepts. The authors further cleaned their data after viewing these initial concept maps and finding a number of irrelevant terms then used Leximancer to analyze the concept of nursing in terms of its co-occurrence with other concepts.

Analysis of Texts as Social Information

Another form of sociological text analysis treats texts as reflections of the practical knowledge of their authors. This type of analysis is prevalent in grounded theory studies as well as in applied studies of expert discourses. Interest in the informative analysis of texts is due in part to its practical value because user-generated texts can potentially provide social scientists and applied researchers with reliable information about social reality. Naturally, the quality of information about social reality that is contained in texts varies according to the level of knowledge of each individual who has participated in the creation of the text, and the information that subjects provide is partial insofar as it is filtered by their own particular point of view. So in addition to their informative components, texts also include ideological components.

An example of analysis of texts as social information is a 2012 psychological study by Colley and Neal on the topic of organizational safety, starting with small representative samples of upper managers, supervisors, and workers in an Australian freight and passenger rail company. Colley and Neal conducted open-ended interviews with members of the three groups that were transcribed and analyzed using Leximancer for map analysis (see Chapter 7). Comparing the concept maps produced for the three groups revealed that the "safety climate schema" of upper managers, supervisors, and workers differed significantly.

Text Mining Fundamentals

PART II

3

Web Crawling
and Scraping

Learning Objectives

The goals of Chapter 3 are to help readers do the following:

1. Understand the basic organization of the web and learn about estimates of its size.

2. Learn about the main techniques for web crawling and scraping.

3. Learn about available software packages for automatically collecting textual data from webpages.

The web—a common abbreviation for the World Wide Web—consists of billions of interlinked hypertext pages. These pages contain text, images, videos, or sounds and are usually viewed using web browsers such as Firefox or Internet Explorer. Users can navigate the web either by directly typing the address of a webpage (the URL) inside a browser or by following the links that connect webpages between them.

In this chapter, we review Internet-based methods for crawling and scraping document collections for social science research. While these two terms are often used interchangeably, we use *crawling* to refer to the process of automatically identifying (via link navigation) the webpages that should be included in a collection and *scraping* to refer to the process of extracting the text from a collection of webpages.

The web can be visualized as a typical example of a graph, with webpages corresponding to vertices in the graph and links between pages corresponding to directed edges. For instance, if the page http://www.umich.edu includes a link to the page http://www.eecs.umich.edu and one to the page http://med.umich.edu, and the later page in turn links to the page of the National Institutes of Health (http://www.nih.gov) and also back to the http://www.umich.edu page, it means that these four pages form a subgraph of four vertices with four edges, as is illustrated in Figure 3.1.

In addition to "traditional" webpages, which account for a large fraction of the data that we currently find online, today's web also includes a number of other data sources, such as sites with user-contributed content (e.g., Wikipedia, Huffington Post), social media sites (e.g., Twitter, Facebook, Blogger), deep web data (e.g., data stored in online databases such as data.gov), or e-mail (e.g., Gmail, Outlook). While

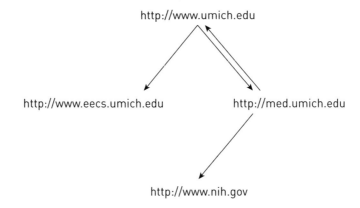

some of these sources may not be publicly available (for instance, e-mail is by definition private and so are a number of Facebook profiles), they still represent data in digital format that accounts for online traffic.

There are many challenges that come with the use of web data—many of which are highlighted in Chapter 13 (see the Web-Based Information Retrieval section). In addition, there are also challenges that are associated with crawling such data, which we address in this chapter.

Web Statistics

While the size of the web is generally considered to be unknown, there are various estimates concerning the size of the indexed web—that is, the subset of the web that is covered by search engines. Web statistics compiled in 2014 by http://www.geekwire .com suggested 5 million terabytes of data online, out of which approximately 20% is textual data.

The web is estimated to include more than 600 million web servers and 2.4 billion web users, which includes about 1 billion Facebook users and 200 million Twitter users (http://royal.pingdom.com/2013/01/16/internet-2012-in-numbers). Estimates of the number of e-mails come from http://www.radicati.com, which suggests that 154 billion e-mails are sent daily, of which more than 60% are spam.

An interesting statistic refers to the proportion of languages used on the web. Information collected by http://www.internetworldstats.com in 2015 showed the distribution of language use as illustrated in Figure 3.2.

FIGURE 3.2 ● Top Ten Languages on the Web in 2015

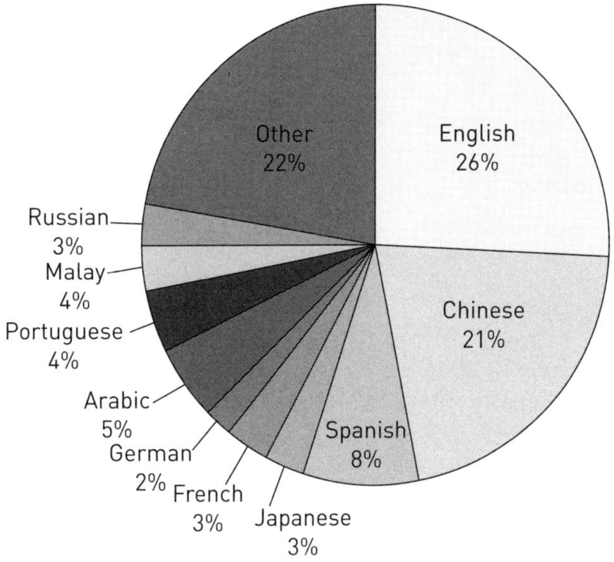

Source: http://www.internetworldstats.com/stats7.htm

Web Crawling

Web crawling is the process of building a collection of webpages by starting with an initial set of URLs (or links) and recursively traversing the corresponding pages to find additional links. A collection built this way can be used, for instance, to create an index for a search engine (see Chapter 13) and to perform information extraction (IE) and text mining (Chapter 12), text classification (Chapter 11), or any other process that requires textual data.

Processing Steps in Crawling

A crawler typically performs the following steps.

1. The crawler creates and maintains a list of URLs to be processed. This list is initially seeded with some manually selected URLs, and it is then iteratively grown into a large set of URLs.
2. The crawler selects a URL from the list (see below for selection strategies), marks it as "crawled," and it fetches the webpage from that URL. The page is processed, and links and content are extracted. This processing can be as simple as just extracting links using a regular expression that matches all the occurrences of

tags such as ←a href="http://...."→, followed by removal of all the HTML tags to obtain the content of the page. At times, a more sophisticated processing may be required, for instance when the links also include relative links or links to fragments or when the content of a page includes entire sections devoted to advertisements or other content that needs to be removed.

3. If the content has already been seen, it is discarded. If not, it is added to the collection of webpages to be further processed (e.g., indexed, classified, etc.)

4. For each URL in the new set of URLs identified on the page, a verification is made to ensure that the URL has not been seen before, that the page exists, and that it can be crawled. If all these filters are passed, the URL is added to the list of URLs at step 1, and the crawler goes back to step 2.

Traversal Strategies

An important aspect of any crawler is its web traversal strategies. As mentioned before, the web is a graph, and therefore, different graph traversal algorithms can be applied. One way of traversing the web is called breadth-first, where, given one webpage, we first collect and process all the pages that can be reached from URLs on that page before we move on to other pages. The second way of traversing the web is called depth-first, where, given one webpage, we extract one URL from that page, collect and process the page that can be reached from that one URL, extract again one URL on the page we just processed, and so on until we reach a "dead end." Only then do we backtrack and process additional URLs on the pages we have just visited. For instance, Figure 3.3 shows a simple web graph, along with the order of page traversal, starting with page A, for each of these two strategies.

Crawler Politeness

Most websites have a clear crawling policy that states which crawlers can or cannot traverse them and which parts of the site can be crawled. There are two main ways of indicating a crawling policy. The most commonly used one is robots.txt, which is a

---

FIGURE 3.3 ● Web Traversal Strategies

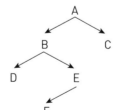

Breadth-first traversal order: A, B, C, D, E, F
Depth-first traversal order: A, B, D, E, F, C

file that is placed at the root of the website (e.g., http://www.cnn.com/robots.txt). This file can include a list of crawlers (or agents) that are disallowed for specific portions of the site. For instance, the following content of robots.txt indicates that all the crawlers are disallowed from traversing pages found under /tmp or /cgi-bin, and BadBot is disallowed from the entire site:

User-agent: *

Disallow: /tmp/

Disallow: /cgi-bin/

User-agent: BadBot

Disallow: /

Another way of providing a crawling policy is through meta tags included in the HTML of individual pages. There is a special meta tag called "robots," which can be used with combinations of values for two aspects: index or noindex (allow or disallow this webpage to be crawled), and follow or nofollow (allow or disallow the crawler to follow links on this webpage). For instance, a webpage could have a robots meta tag as follows:

←meta name="robots" content="index,nofollow"→

It states that this page can be crawled, but links on the page cannot be followed.

Writing a crawler requires some basic programming knowledge. Starting with a set of input URLs, the program will perform the four steps described previously to grow the collection of URLs. Alternatively, one can also use existing commands—for instance, the Linux command wget, which allows for recursive crawling with a prespecified depth of the crawl.

Web Scraping

Web scraping is used to extract text from webpages, be they pages that have been identified through crawling (e.g., all the pages found under a given website) or pages in digital archives, including news archives such as LexisNexis (http://www.lexisnexis .com) and Access World News (http://www.newsbank.com/libraries/schools/solutions/ us-international/access-world-news) as well as digital archives of historical documents (Jockers & Mimno, 2013).

Web scraping software is designed to recognize different types of content within a website and to acquire and store only the types of content specified by the user. For instance, web scraping software allows a user to search a newspaper website and save only the names of article authors or to search a real estate website and save only the prices, addresses, or descriptions of listed properties.

Scraping involves using commercial software or programming languages such as Python, Java, or Perl to write programs for scraping "from scratch" or to write programs that make use of existing application program interfaces (APIs). The goal of web scraping is to identify the "useful" text within webpages. While text comes in many forms, the "usefulness" of the text to be gathered via scraping is defined by the needs of a project. For instance, if the goal is to build a collection of news stories, one would want to identify the text of the news articles included in the webpages found by a crawler on websites such as www.cnn.com or www.nbcnews.com, and at the same time, it will want to identify and ignore the text of the advertisements found on the same webpages.

Scraping from scratch (i.e., by using a programming language) involves a process of reversed engineering of the webpage structure, along with the use of regular expressions. Starting with one (or few) of the target webpages, the programmer of the web scraper will first look closely at the source of the webpage, using the Page Source menu option found under regular web browsers such as Firefox or Internet Explorer. The inspection of the page source will allow the programmer to identify patterns that can be used to locate the useful text. For instance, she could find that the text of the news articles of interest is surrounded by tags such as <article> . . . </article> or that the title of an article is marked by <h2> . . . </h2> tags that immediately follow a </date> tag. These patterns can then be used to write regular expressions in the programming language of choice which, when applied on a target webpage, will result in the desired text.

There are also websites that provide APIs, which also assume a minimum amount of programming knowledge but do not require the reverse engineering process described previously. The APIs define the structure of the data that can be extracted (or scraped) from a site and provide an easy interface to access this data. The use of APIs requires the programmer to first read the documentation of the API to understand what data is accessible via the API and how the API can be used. For instance, the following are two examples of APIs: the Twitter API https://dev.twitter.com/overview/api to access tweets based through search or as random subsets of the existing tweets; the Blogger API, https://developers.google.com/blogger/?hl=en to access the profile of the bloggers and the content of the blogs available on Google Blogger. It is important to note that many of these APIs have usage restrictions (e.g., the Blogger API requires an API key and restricts the access to a certain number of requests per day).

Commercial web scraping software is also available, and it is reasonably easy to use for nonprogrammers. The software works by running "scripts" written by the user. The scripts tell the software on which webpage to start, what kind of text to look for (e.g., text with a certain font size or formatting), what to do with the text that is found, where to navigate next once text is saved, and how many times to repeat the script. Saved text data can be downloaded in a convenient file form such as raw text, or a CSV (comma-separated values) file.

There are several useful freeware and commercial software products available on the market, and instructional videos for most of these are easy to find on YouTube and other Internet video services or in the manual pages available on Linux via the *man* command. In our own research, we have used Lynx, which is a very simple Linux-based command-line browser that allows for automatic processing of a page, including link and content extraction. We have also used Helium Scraper (http://www.heliumscraper.com).

Software for Web Crawling and Scraping

Web crawling can be effectively performed using publicly available implementations such as the following:

- Scrapy (http://scrapy.org), a collection of Python scripts
- LWP (http://search.cpan.org/dist/libwww-perl/lib/LWP.pm), a Perl library

The following packages can be used for scraping:

- Helium Scraper (http://www.heliumscraper.com)
- Outwit (http://www.outwit.com)
- Outwit Hub (https://www.outwit.com/products/hub)
- FMiner (http://www.fminer.com)
- Mozenda (https://www.mozenda.com)
- Visual Web Ripper (http://www.visualwebripper.com)

For data collection from social media, it is typical to use the publicly available APIs made available by the social media platforms, such as the following:

- Twitter API (https://dev.twitter.com/overview/api), which can be used to search Twitter data or access their public stream of recent tweets
- Google Blogger API (https://developers.google.com/blogger/?hl=en), which provides access to the blogs and blogger profiles published on Blogger (https://www.blogger.com)

4

Lexical Resources

●
Learning Objectives

The goals of Chapter 4 are to help readers do the following:

1. Learn about the representation and content of several lexical resources.
2. Learn about downloadable lexical resources and available software packages to access lexical resources.

A lexical resource is a collection of lexical items (i.e., words or phrases) with some additional linguistic information. A typical instance of a lexical resource is a dictionary, which lists words along with definitions and usage examples. Another example of a lexical resource is a thesaurus, which groups related words together. Yet another example is a collection of words or phrases mapped to a set of semantic classes (e.g., *family* or *positive emotions*).

Lexical resources play an important role in most text mining applications. For instance, lexical resources are used in the development of text processing tools (Chapter 5), can be used for metaphor analysis (Chapter 9), form the foundations for many word and text relatedness methods (Chapter 10), can be used to generate features for text classification and sentiment analysis (Chapters 11 and 14), and can support methods for information extraction (IE; Chapter 12) and information retrieval (Chapter 13). The development of lexical resources is usually labor intensive, as it requires a significant amount of time from experts such as lexicographers (aka dictionary makers; e.g., WordNet) or psychologists (e.g., Lexical Inquiry and Word Count). Some resources took many years to complete, and many resources went through several versions over time. More recently constructed lexical resources (e.g., Wikipedia or Wiktionary) took advantage of crowdsourcing, which comes with the advantage of a significantly larger number of contributors at the cost of consistency (and sometimes at the cost of quality).

WordNet

WordNet (Fellbaum, 1998; Miller, 1995) is an electronic semantic network started in 1985 by a group led by George Miller at Princeton University. WordNet covers the majority of nouns, verbs, adjectives, and adverbs in the English language, along with a rich set of semantic relations that connect these concepts. Words in WordNet are

TABLE 4.1 ● Semantic Relations in WordNet

Relation	Description	Example
Hypernym (nouns, verbs)	A is a hypernym of B means B is an A.	*Canine* is a hypernym of *dog*.
Hyponyms (nouns, verbs)	A is a hyponym of B means A is a B.	*Dalmatian* is a hyponym of *dog*.
Holonyms (nouns)	A is a holonym of B means B is part of A.	*Tree* is a holonym of *trunk*.
Meronyms (nouns)	A is a meronym of B means A is part of B.	*Bark* is a meronym of *trunk*.
Coordinates (nouns, verbs)	A is a coordinate of B means A and B have a common hypernym.	*Dalmatian* is a coordinate of *poodle* (they both have *dog* as a hypernym).
Troponym (verbs)	A is a troponym of B means doing A is a manner of doing B.	*To march* is a troponym of *to walk*.
Entailment (verbs)	A entails B means doing A implies also doing B.	*To snore* entails *to sleep*.
Related nouns (adjectives)	A has related noun B means A was derived from B.	*Studious* has related noun *study*.
Antonym (adjectives, adverbs)	A is an antonym of B means A and B have opposite meanings.	*Beautiful* is an antonym of *ugly*.
Similar to (adjectives)	A is similar to B means A and B have similar meanings.	*Beautiful* is similar to *lovely*.

organized in synonym sets, also called *synsets*. WordNet 3.1 is the latest WordNet version (as of June 2015), and it has a large network of 155,000 words grouped into 117,000 synsets.

Many of the synsets in WordNet are connected to several other synsets via semantic relations, such as hypernymy ("is a"), homonymy ("part of"), and so on. Table 4.1 lists the semantic relations available in WordNet, together with examples.

Nouns and verbs are organized into hierarchies, based on the hypernymy/hyponymy relation. Figure 4.1 shows a snapshot of a WordNet noun hierarchy.

Adjectives and nouns are organized into clusters of related words, often with cluster heads that are found in an antonymy relation. Figure 4.2 shows a snapshot of an adjective cluster in WordNet.

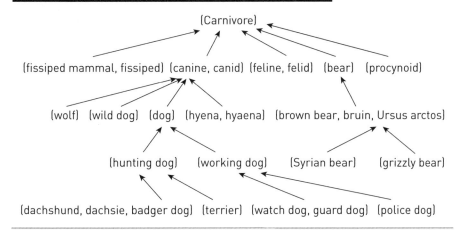

FIGURE 4.1 ● Snapshot of a WordNet Noun Hierarchy

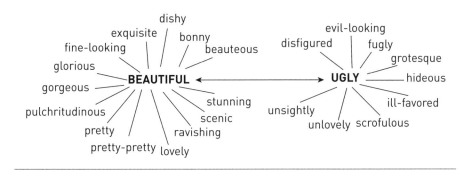

FIGURE 4.2 ● Snapshot of a WordNet Adjective Cluster

WordNet-Affect

WordNet-Affect (Strapparava & Valitutti, 2004) is a resource that was created starting with WordNet by annotating synsets with several emotions. It uses several resources for affective information, including the emotion classification of Ortony, Clore, and Foss (1987). WordNet-Affect was constructed in two stages. First, a core resource was built based on a number of heuristics and semiautomatic processing, followed by a second stage where the core synsets were automatically expanded using the semantic relations available in WordNet.

Table 4.2 shows several sample words for each of the six basic emotions of Ortony: anger, disgust, fear, joy, sadness, and surprise.

TABLE 4.2 ● Sample Words From WordNet-Affect	
Emotion	**Sample Words**
anger	wrath, umbrage, offense, temper, irritation, lividity, irascibility, fury, rage
disgust	horror, foul, disgust, abominably, hideous, sick, tired of, wicked, yucky
fear	terrible, ugly, unsure, unkind, timid, scar, outrageous, panic, hysteria, intimidated
joy	worship, adoration, sympathy, tenderness, regard, respect, pride, preference, love
sadness	aggrieve, misery, oppressive, pathetic, tearful, sorry, gloomy, dismay
surprise	wonder, awe, amazement, astounding, stupefying, dazed, stunned, amazingly

Roget's Thesaurus

Roget's Thesaurus (Roget, 1987) is a thesaurus of the English language, with words and phrases grouped into hierarchical classes. A word class usually includes synonyms, as well as other words that are semantically related. Classes are typically divided into sections, subsections, heads and paragraphs, which are in turn divided by part of speech: nouns, verbs, adjectives, and adverbs. Finally, each paragraph is grouped into several sets of semantically related words. The version of *Roget's Thesaurus* that is publicly available for research use is the 1911 original Roget version, and it includes about 250,000 words, grouped into eight broad classes that branch into 39 sections, 79 subsections, 596 head groups, and finally 990 heads.

Table 4.3 shows four sample word sets found under each of the four parts of speech under the head Informality.

Linguistic Inquiry and Word Count

Linguistic Inquiry and Word Count (LIWC) was developed as a resource for psycholinguistic analysis, by Pennebaker and colleagues (Pennebaker, Francis, & Booth, 2001; Pennebaker & King, 1999). It has been used in a large number of studies in social, psychological, and linguistic research, addressing tasks such as analysis of psychology traits (Mairesse, Walker, Mehl, & Moore, 2007; Pennebaker & King, 1999), deception (Mihalcea & Strapparava, 2009; Ott, Choi, Cardie, & Hancock, 2011), social analysis of conversations (Stark, Shafran, & Kaye, 2012), prediction of depression (Resnik, Garron, & Resnik, 2013), identification of sarcasm (González-Ibánez, Muresan, & Wacholder, 2011), and many others.

TABLE 4.3 ● Sample Word Sets for the Word *Informality* in *Roget's Thesaurus*	
Part of Speech	**Sample Set of Semantically Related Words**
noun	informality, informalness, lack of formality, lack of ceremony, unceremoniousness, lack of convention, indifference, noncomformity, casualness, offhandedness
verb	be informal, not stand on ceremony, be oneself, be natural, relax, feel at home, make oneself at home, not insist, waive the rules, come as you are, let one's hair down
adjective	familiar, natural, simple, plain, unpretentious, homely, folksy, common, unaffected
adverb	freely, indulgently, tolerantly, unconstrainedly, permissively, loosely, irregularly

Source: Roget (1987).

The 2007 version of LIWC includes more than 2,000 words and word stems grouped into close to 80 word categories. The word categories are grouped into four broad classes: linguistic processes, covering primarily function words and other common words; psychological processes, including social, affective, cognitive, perceptual, biological, and time processes; personal concerns, such as work, money, and religion; and spoken categories, including fillers and other spoken words. The LIWC lexicon has been validated by showing significant correlation between human ratings of a large number of written texts and the rating obtained through LIWC-based analyses of the same texts.

Table 4.4 shows four LIWC categories along with a set of sample words included in these classes.

TABLE 4.4 ● Three Sample Linguistic Inquiry and Word Count Classes With Sample Words		
Category	**Class**	**Sample Words**
We	Linguistic processes	our, ourselves, we, we'd, we'll, us, let's, we've, we're, lets
Achievement	Personal concerns	better, award, ahead, advance, achieve, motivate, lose, honor, climb, first, fail
Nonfluencies	Spoken categories	er, umm, uh, um, zz

Source: Pennebaker et al. (2001).

TABLE 4.5 • Sample Categories and Words in General Inquirer	
Category	**Sample Words**
Academ[ic]	academic, astronomy, biology, chemistry, credit, dean, degree, physician, library
Ritual	ambush, appointment, affair, bridge, census, commemorate, debut, demonstration
Female	aunt, feminine, girl, goddess, her, heroine, grandmother, mother, queen, she

Source: Stone and Hunt (1963).

General Inquirer

The General Inquirer (Stone & Hunt, 1963) is a dictionary of about 10,000 words grouped into about 100 categories. Similar to LIWC, the classes defined in the General Inquirer have social and psycholinguistic motivations and has been widely used for content analysis. Three General Inquirer categories are shown in Table 4.5, together with sample words from these categories.

Wikipedia

Wikipedia is a free online encyclopedia, representing the outcome of a continuous collaborative effort of a large number of volunteer contributors. Virtually any Internet user can create or edit a Wikipedia webpage, and this "freedom of contribution" has a positive impact on both the quantity (fast-growing number of articles) and the quality (potential mistakes are quickly corrected within the collaborative environment) of this online resource.

While some may argue that Wikipedia in its raw form is not a lexical resource, this online encyclopedia includes a significant amount of linguistic information that can be compiled into lexical resources. For instance, similar to a dictionary, words and phrases in Wikipedia are linked to their definitional articles. Synonymy relations can be inferred by extracting all the words and phrases that link to a certain article. Moreover, Wikipedia is also a rich resource for cross-lingual relations, as articles defining the same concept in different languages are explicitly linked.

The basic entry in Wikipedia is an article (or page) that defines and describes a concept, an entity, or an event and consists of a hypertext document with hyperlinks to other pages within or outside Wikipedia. The role of the hyperlinks is to guide the reader to pages that provide additional information about the entities or events mentioned in an article. Articles are organized into categories, which in turn are organized into category hierarchies. For instance, the article on Alan Turing shown partially in Figure 4.3 is included in the category British cryptographers, which in turn has a parent category named British scientists and so forth.

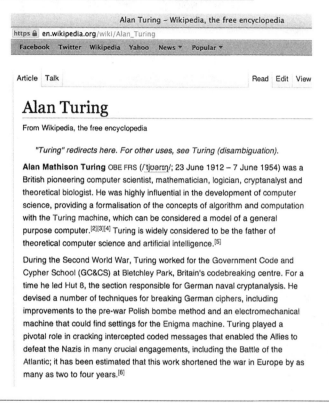

FIGURE 4.3 ● **Snapshot of a Sample Wikipedia Page**

Source: Wikipedia (n.d.).

Each article in Wikipedia is uniquely referenced by an identifier, consisting of one or more words separated by spaces or underscores and occasionally a parenthetical explanation. For example, the article for the entity *Turing* that refers to the "English computer scientist" has the unique identifier *Alan Turing*, whereas the article on Turing with the "stream cipher" meaning has the unique identifier *Turing* (cipher).

The hyperlinks within Wikipedia are created using these unique identifiers, together with an anchor text that represents the surface form of the hyperlink. For instance, "Alan Mathison Turing, [OBE], [FRS], . . . was British pioneering [computer scientist], [mathematician], [logician], [cryptanalyst] and [theoretical biologist]" is the wiki source for the first sentence in the example page on Alan Turing in Figure 4.3, containing links to the articles Officer of the Order of the British Empire, Fellow of the Royal Society, Computer scientist, Mathematician, Logician, Cryptanalysis, and Mathematical and theoretical biology.

One of the implications of the large number of contributors editing the Wikipedia articles is the occasional lack of consistency with respect to the unique identifier used for a certain entity. For instance, Alan Turing is also referred to using the last name Turing, or the full name Alan Mathison Turing. This has led to the so-called redirect pages, which consist of a redirection hyperlink from an alternative name (e.g., Turing) to the article actually containing the description of the entity (e.g., Alan Turing). Another structure that is worth mentioning is the disambiguation page. Disambiguation pages are specifically created for ambiguous entities and consist of links to articles defining the different meanings of the entity. The unique identifier for a disambiguation page typically consists of the parenthetical explanation (disambiguation) attached to the name of the ambiguous entity, as in for example, Sense_(disambiguation), which is the unique identifier for the disambiguation page of the noun *sense*.

Wikipedia editions are available for more than 280 languages, with a number of entries varying from a few pages to 5 million articles or more per language. Table 4.6 shows the 10 largest Wikipedias (as of January 2016), along with the number of articles and approximate number of users for each.

Also worth noting are the interlingual links, which explicitly connect articles in different languages. For instance, the English article for the noun *sense* is connected, among others, to the Spanish article *sentido (percepcion)*, and the Latin article *sensus*

TABLE 4.6 ● Number of Articles and Users for the Top Ten Wikipedia Editions From http://meta.wikimedia.org/wiki/List_of_Wikipedias

Language	Wiki	Articles	Users
English	en	5,051,365	27,188,205
Swedish	sv	2,510,531	473,024
German	de	1,894,815	2,327,273
Dutch	nl	1,850,356	740,674
Cebuano	ceb	1,786,025	24,686
French	fr	1,713,034	2,416,197
Russian	ru	1,280,569	1,824,550
Waray-Waray	war	1,259,441	27,109
Italian	it	1,246,036	1,312,384
Spanish	es	1,224,435	4,056,965
Polish	pl	1,151,399	730,193
Vietnamese	vi	1,142,145	476,707

Source: List of Wikipedias (n.d.).

(biologia). On average, about half of the articles in a Wikipedia version include interlingual links to articles in other languages. The number of interlingual links per article varies from an average of 5 in the English Wikipedia, to 10 in the Spanish Wikipedia, and as many as 23 in the Arabic Wikipedia.

Wiktionary

A sister project of Wikipedia, run by the same Wikimedia Foundation, Wiktionary is a volunteer contributed dictionary, covering a large number of languages. Words in Wiktionary include synonyms and definitions, connections to translations in other languages, and a number of relations such as hyponyms ("is a") and derived terms. A useful piece of information that is available for many words in Wiktionary is the etymology of the words, which connects the current form of a word to earlier versions sometimes in other languages.

Downloadable Lexical Resources and Application Program Interfaces

Several of the lexical resources described in this chapter are publicly available, and several of them also have application program interfaces (APIs) available for use. WordNet is available at http://wordnet.princeton.edu, which also includes a link to an online interface, a downloadable database, and a number of APIs. WordNet-Affect is available from http://wndomains.fbk.eu/wnaffect.html. The 1911 version of the *Roget's Thesaurus* is in the public domain and can be downloaded from a number of sites including Gutenberg (http://www.gutenberg.org/etext/22). The newer version of *Roget's Thesaurus* is not publicly available, and while it can be accessed online at http://www.thesaurus.com, one needs to purchase access to the full resource. LIWC can be tested online or purchased from http://liwc.wpengine.com. The General Inquirer can be obtained from http://www.wjh.harvard.edu/~inquirer. Copies of Wikipedia or Wiktionary in various languages can be downloaded as a dump from https://dumps.wikimedia.org/backup-index.html.

5

Basic Text Processing

Learning Objectives

The goals of Chapter 5 are to help readers do the following:

1. Understand some of the basic text processing steps, such as tokenization, stop word removal, stemming, and lemmatization.
2. Learn about text statistics and laws that govern the distribution of words in text.
3. Understand the basics of language models, and learn about their applications.
4. Understand the main goals of more advanced text processing steps.

Text analysis almost invariably requires some form of text processing. It can consist of more basic steps such as removing the HyperText Markup Language (HTML) tags from a group of documents collected from the web, separating the punctuation from the words, removing function words, and applying stemming or lemmatization. It can also take more advanced forms such as annotating text with part of speech tags or syntactic dependency trees as well as other layers of annotations such as mapping words to senses in a dictionary or finding discourse markers. This chapter covers some of the basic text processing steps, including tokenization, stop word removal, lemmatization and stemming, text statistics, and language models. It also provides pointers for additional reading for the more advanced text processing.

Basic text processing is often the first step in research studies that involve linguistic input. Oftentimes, it is sufficient to just remove extraneous tags (e.g., HTML, Extensible Markup Language [XML]) and tokenize the punctuation, which will result in a set of tokens that can be used to collect statistics or to use as input for other applications such as sentiment analysis or text classification. But there are also times when it is useful to remove the very frequent words (through stop word removal) or obtain the root form of the words (through stemming or lemmatization). The kind of text processing steps that are to be applied is often application dependent: If one wants, for instance, to analyze the language of deception, stop words are useful and should be preserved, but if the goal is to separate computer science texts from biology texts, then stop words can be removed, and one may also benefit from stemming all the input words. There can also be cases when one is interested in identifying all the organizations that appear in a corpus, in which case it is beneficial to have available more advanced annotations such as the ones provided by a named entity recognition tool.

Tokenization

Tokenization is the process of identifying the words in the input sequence of characters, mainly by separating the punctuation marks but also by identifying contractions, abbreviations, and so forth. For instance, given the text "Mr. Smith doesn't like apples," we would like output that has each word as a separate token, as in "Mr. Smith does n't like apples." Tokenization may seem like a trivial process at first, but there are some cases that require special attention. For instance, for a period, we need to distinguish between end-of-sentence periods and markers of abbreviations (e.g., Mr., Dr., U.S.). While we do want to separate the end of the sentence from the word before, it is preferred to keep the period attached to the abbreviations, as they are words that require the period to be well formed. The period also has special meaning and should be kept as is inside numbers (e.g., 12.4) or dates (e.g., 12.05.2015) or IP addresses (e.g., 100.2.34.58).

- For an apostrophe, we often want to identify the contractions and separate them such that they form meaningful individual words. For instance, the possessive *books'* should form two words: *book* and *s'*. The contractions *aren't* and *he's* should be separated into *are* and *n't* and *he* and *'s*.
- Quotations should also be separated from the text, as in, for example, "Let it be", which should become " Let it be ".
- For hyphenations, we often leave them in place, to indicate a collocation as in, for example, *state-of-the-art*, although sometimes it may be useful to separate it, to allow for access to individual words—for example, separate *Hewlett-Packard* into *Hewlett - Packard*.

While tokenization is largely language independent, several of the special cases that need to be handled for correct tokenization can be language specific. For instance, abbreviations and contractions are often dependent on language, and thus, one needs to compile a list of such words to make sure that the tokenization of the period is handled correctly. The same applies to apostrophe and hyphenation.

Sometimes the tokenization process also includes other text normalization steps, such as lowercasing or the more advanced truecasing (e.g., selecting the correct case for the words *apple* in "There is an apple symbol on my Apple Macbook"), or removal of HTML tags, if the text is obtained from a webpage.

Note that the process of tokenization assumes that white spaces and punctuation are used as explicit word boundaries. This is the case with many of the languages that use a Latin alphabet, as well as several other language families, but it is not the case with most Asian languages. Processing an input source of characters in an Asian language also requires a separate step of word boundary detection, which is often done using supervised learning algorithms. There are also languages that make heavy use of compound words such as German (Computerlinguistik means "computational linguistics"), or agglutinative languages such as Inuktitut (Tusaatsiarunnanngittualuujunga means "I can't hear very well").

Stop Word Removal

Stop words, also referred to as function words or closed-class words, consist of high-frequency words including pronouns (e.g., *I*, *we*, *us*), determiners (e.g., *the*, *a*), prepositions (e.g., *in*, *on*), and others. For some tasks, stop words can be useful: For instance, it has been found that they can give significant insights into people's personalities and behaviors (Mihalcea & Strapparava 2009; Pennebaker & King, 1999). But there are also tasks when it is useful to remove them and focus the attention on content words such as nouns and verbs. Whatever the case, it is important to have the means to identify the stop words in an input text. In general, this is done using a precompiled list of stop words together with an efficient lookup algorithm.

Stop words are clearly language-dependent, and thus, an important question is how to create a list of stop words for the language of interest. Well-studied languages, such as English or Spanish or Chinese, have several such lists publicly available. If a list of stop words is not available for a given language, relying on the fact that stop words are high-frequency words (see the following section), one can gather word statistics on a very large corpus of texts written in that language and consequently get the top N most frequent words as candidate stop words. Ideally, the corpus should contain a mix of texts from different domains to avoid high frequency for some words due to their domain specificity (e.g., a collection of texts on computer science will inherently include the word *computer* with high frequency). It is a good practice to also get the feedback of a native speaker on the list of candidate stop words, as sometimes it can also include words that are frequent but are not stop words (e.g., *have*, *get*, *today*).

Stemming and Lemmatization

Many words in natural language are related, yet they have different surface forms, which makes their recognition nontrivial. While some of these relations are of semantic nature and require dictionary knowledge, as in for example, *sick* and *ill*, there are also many relations that can be more easily captured through simpler forms of string analysis, as is the case with *construction* and *construct* or *water* and *watered*.

The simplest way to identify the common stem of multiple words is through the process called stemming. Simply put, stemming applies a set of rules to an input word to remove suffixes and prefixes and obtain its stem, which will now be shared with other related words. For instance, *computer*, *computational*, and *computation* will be all reduced to the same stem: *compute*.

Stemming often produces stems that are not valid words, which is irrelevant if the "consumer" of these stems is a system and not a human. For instance, stemming is used in information retrieval (see Chapter 13), where the stems are fed into the index-ing process and improve the quality of the information retrieval system, without ever being read by the users of that system. Stemming, however, should not be used if the stemmed text is to be read by a human, as oftentimes it is hard to understand. Consider, for example, the text "for example compressed and compression are both accepted as equivalent to compress," which a stemmer will transform into "for exampl compres and compres are both accept as equival to compres."

There are many stemmers out there, the most popular one being the Porter Stemmer, which is a simple procedure for removing known affixes in English with-out using a dictionary. The Porter Stemmer consists of a set of transformation rules, such as *sses → ss, ies → i, ational → ate, tional → tion*, which are applied repeatedly on a word until no transformations are obtained. The stemmer was found to work well in evaluations performed in information retrieval systems, where the quality of the retrieval system was improved when applied on stemmed text. It also makes errors, including errors of "comission," such as *organization* and *organ* being both stemmed to *organ* or *police* and *policy* sharing the stem *polic*, or errors of "omission," such as *cylinder* and *cylindrical* or *Europe* and *European* not being stemmed at all. The stemmer is clearly language dependent, but versions of the stemmer for several languages other than English also exist.

The alternative to stemming is lemmatization, which reduces the inflectional forms of a word to its root form. For instance, lemmatization will transform *boys* to *boy*; *children* to *child*; and *am, are* or *is* to *be*. Unlike stemming, the output obtained from lemmatization is a valid word form, which is the base form of a word as found in a dictionary. Thus, lemmatization has the benefit that its output is readable by humans; however, this comes at a cost of a more computationally intensive process, as it requires a list of grammatical forms to handle the regular inflections as well as an extensive list of irregular words.

Text Statistics

One of the simplest analyses that one can do on any collection of text is to count words and determine what are the words that occur with higher frequency. Interestingly, despite its complexity, natural language is very predictable: One can, for instance, make a good guess as to what will be the most frequent words in any text collection or make predictions as to what will be the size of the vocabulary (i.e., number of unique words) in a new collection.

For instance, Table 5.1 shows the top 10 most frequent words in one of the benchmark collections from the Text Retrieval Conference (TREC-3). As seen in this table, the most frequent words are generally stop words, as also mentioned in the previous section.

If we plot the frequency of words in a corpus, we generally obtain a curve that looks like the one shown in Figure 5.1.

TABLE 5.1 ● Word Frequencies in TREC-3 (125,720,891 total words, 508,209 unique words. From B. Croft)		
Frequent Word	Number Occurrences	Percentage of Total
the	7,398,934	5.9
of	3,893,790	3.1
to	3,364,653	2.7
and	3,320,687	2.6
in	2,311,785	1.8
is	1,559,147	1.2
for	1,313,561	1.0
The	1,144,860	0.9
that	1,066,503	0.8
said	1,027,713	0.8

FIGURE 5.1 ● Distribution of Word Frequencies in a Corpus

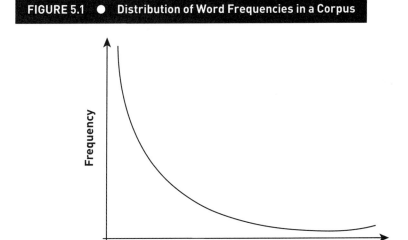

What this curve shows is that there are a few words that are very common. For instance, words such as *the* or *of* can account for as much as 10% of all the word occurrences in a collection. At the other end of the curve we have the rare words, which make the "bulk" of the words in a corpus. In fact, it has been shown that half the words in a collection of texts appear only once (these words are called *hapax legomena*, which means "read only once" in Greek).

There are two laws that have been established on word distributions: Zipf's law and Heap's law. Zipf's law models the distribution of terms in a corpus and provides a mathematical way to answer this question: How many times does the rth most frequent word appear in a corpus of N words? Specifically, assuming that f is the frequency of a word, and r is its rank reflecting the position of the word in a list sorted by decreasing frequency (e.g., in Table 5.1, the word *of* has a frequency of 3,893,790 and has rank 2 in the frequency sorted list), Zipf found in 1949 the following:

$$f.r = k \text{ (for constant } k)$$

The constant k depends on the corpus. Zipf's law can be used to make predictions regarding the number of words that have a certain frequency range and generally to show the distribution of words in a corpus.

The second law, called Heap's law, models the number of words in the vocabulary as a function of the corpus size. The number of unique words (vocabulary) in a collection does not grow linearly with number of words in that collection. This is because words that we have already seen will start repeating as the corpus grows, and thus, the shape of vocabulary vs. size that we generally use is shown in Figure 5.2.

Interestingly, the curve never plateaus either, and this is because there are certain word classes in language, such as numbers and proper names, which are endless

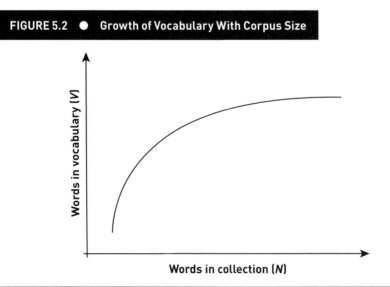

FIGURE 5.2 ● Growth of Vocabulary With Corpus Size

sources of new words. So no matter how large a corpus is (and thus its corresponding vocabulary), adding more text to it will likely bring a few more new words.

Heap's law can be used to answer questions such as the following: What is the number of unique words appearing in a corpus of N words? How many words will I have in a collection when I will have a vocabulary of V words? Given a corpus of N words with a vocabulary of V words, Heap's law states the following:

$$V = Kn^{\beta} \text{ with constants } K, 0 < \beta < 1$$

K and β are parameters that can be determined on a given collection of texts. Using this law, one can make predictions as to what will be the vocabulary of a corpus as it grows. For instance, we may know that a collection of legal texts has 1,000,000 words and a vocabulary of 135,000 words. Heap's law will help us make a prediction of what will be the size of the vocabulary in a future setting when the corpus will grow to, for example, 5,000,000 words.

Language Models

Language models are probabilistic representations of natural language, which can be used as predictive or explicative models. Very briefly, a language model will capture the probability of seeing certain sequences of words or characters. For instance, given that we have already seen the word *dog*, is it more likely that we will see *barks* or *writes*? Language models can thus be used to propose possible alternatives, given a history of previously occurred words—for example, given *dog*, what are possible continuations? Or, they can be used to assess likelihood—for example, what is the likelihood of seeing the sequence *dog barks*?

Language models have a very broad range of applications, ranging from spelling corrections (what are the most likely corrections, given an observed incorrect text), to speech recognition (about all possible texts that could be output from an input utterance, which one is more likely), machine translation (which is the most likely translation, given all possible alternatives), handwriting recognition, language recognition, and so forth.

Language models are built on very large corpora (referred to as training corpora) by calculating probabilities of words or sequences of words on the given text collection. Clearly, the larger the collection, the more accurate the language models. Think, for instance, of predicting the likelihood of seeing the sequence *dog eats* by processing the text from this chapter versus processing the text available in some millions of webpages.

The simplest language models are based on unigrams, where we have probabilities associated with individual words. In these models, we mainly count the frequency of individual words and calculate their probability with respect to the entire set of words in the training corpus. For instance, if we have a collection of 100 words, out of which 2 are *dog*, the probability of seeing this individual word (or unigram) is P(dog) = 2/100.

The next stage is to create bigram language models. We now measure the probability of a word given the word before $P(W_i| W_{i-1})$, which can be calculated as $Count(W_{i-1} W_i)/Count(W_{i-1})$. For instance, we could calculate $P(barks|dog)$ as the number of times we have seen *dog barks* divided by the number of times we have seen *dog*.

Next are trigram models, where we estimate $P(W_i| W_{i-1} W_{i-2})$, then four-grams, where we estimate $P(W_i| W_{i-1} W_{i-2} W_{i-3})$, and so forth. The higher the order of the n-gram models, the better the accuracy of the models, as measured through their predictive or explicative power, although sometime overfitting can also occur. The trade-off, however, stands in the amount of data required to train such models, with higher order n-grams requiring significantly larger training sets to avoid data sparseness. Think, for instance, of calculating individual word probabilities from a corpus of 1 million words, versus calculating the probability of sequences of six words at a time (six-grams) from the same corpus. It is likely that we would have seen a lot of the individual words in this corpus, but it is also likely that we have not seen most of the possible sequences of six words in that same corpus. The effect of that is that we will have a lot of zero counts in our six-gram probability estimates, and therefore, the model will end up not being accurate.

Given such language models, we can then combine them to make predictions for entire texts. For instance, if we have the text "I want to eat Chinese food," assuming a bigram model, we can calculate P(I want to eat British food) = P(I|start) P(want|I) P(to|want) P(eat|to) P(British|eat) P(food|British). Similarly, with a trigram model, we would calculate P(I | start start) P (want | start I) P(to|I want) P(eat|want to) P(British|to eat) P(food|eat British), and so forth.

Other Text Processing

As stated at the beginning of this chapter, in addition to basic processing steps, there are other text processing layers that can be applied on any given text. Some of the most commonly used are as follows.

Part of Speech Tagging

Part of speech tagging has the goal to identify the part of speech for any input word. Most of the algorithms are based on supervised learning and therefore rely on previously annotated data in order to learn how to assign parts of speech to new text. There are also different tag sets that have been proposed, ranging from a handful of tags (e.g., Noun, Verb) to larger tag sets such as the Penn Treebank (Marcus, Marcinkiewicz, & Santorini, 1993), which contains close to 40 different tags (e.g., NN = common noun singular, NNS = common noun plural, NNP = proper noun, NNPS = proper noun plural).

Collocation Identification

Collocation identification has the goal to identify collocations or idioms, such as *mother-in-law* or *kick the bucket*. This is often done by using information theoretic measures that try to identify significant co-occurrences in text, such as mutual information of chi-square (Church & Hanks, 1990).

Syntactic Parsing

Syntactic parsing builds upon raw text, or upon part of speech tagged text, and identifies syntactic relations between constituents in language. Some parsers will produce syntactic trees (Collins, 2003), which can have multiple elements in one syntactic constituent (e.g., identify a noun phrase as being formed by a determiner followed by an adjective followed by a noun); other parsers will mainly output dependencies (Klein & Manning, 2004)—that is, binary relations between elements in the text (e.g., an adjective that has a modifier relation to its noun). The most accurate parsers work by training supervised systems on manually parsed data (such as the Penn Treebank [Marcus et al., 1993]), although there has also been work on building unsupervised parsers, which are particularly appealing when a parser is needed for a new language.

Named Entity Tagging

Named entity tagging aims to identify specific named entities, such as person, location, or organization (Nadeau & Sekine, 2007). Named entity tagging is often seen as a specialized case of information extraction (IE).

Word Sense Disambiguation

Word sense disambiguation maps input words to dictionary senses, either by training on an existing set of annotated word senses (Yarowsky, 1995) or by using unsupervised methods that look for commonalities between a word context and a word sense definition (Lesk, 1986). Recent work in word sense disambiguation has also used lexical resources other than dictionaries, such as Wikipedia (Mihalcea, 2007).

Software for Text Processing

There are several software packages that can be used to perform basic text processing. Among the more widely used ones are the Stanford CoreNLP toolkit (http://stanfordnlp .github.io/CoreNLP), which is a Java package that includes many language analysis tools; NLTK (Natural Language Toolkit; http://www.nltk.org), which is a collection of Python libraries for text processing, also including a variety of document collections and lexical resources; and LingPipe (http://alias-i.com/lingpipe), which is a Java toolkit with many text processing tools and a large number of tutorials for core tasks in natural language processing.

6

Supervised Learning

Learning Objectives

The goals of Chapter 6 are to help readers do the following:

1. Understand the task of supervised learning, and learn about its large range of applications.
2. Learn about feature representation and weighting in supervised learning.
3. Learn about specific learning algorithms: decision trees, nearest neighbors, and support vector machines (SVMs).
4. Understand how to evaluate supervised learning methods.
5. Learn about available software packages for supervised learning.

T he field of machine learning is one of the relatively new fields within artificial intelligence, yet it is also one of the most impactful fields, as it has found applications in a very large number of other domains, within and outside computer science.

Simply put, the task of supervised learning (also referred to as supervised machine learning or sometimes simply as learning) consists of using an automatic system to learn from a history of occurrences of a certain "event" and consequently make predictions about future occurrences of that event.

As an example, consider the task of learning whether it will rain or not. We could imagine a set of previous occurrences of the "rain or not" event, along with some representative attributes (or features), as illustrated in rows 1 through 4 in Table 6.1.

Given these previous occurrences of the rain event, we could imagine a system that could identify an association between sky = overcast, humidity = high, wind = strong and rain and consequently be able to predict that it is likely to rain given the observations from instance 5 in Table 6.1.

The task of machine learning is therefore to learn how to most effectively make such predictions. An event is characterized by a set of features or attributes and a class. These are very specific to the task being solved: For instance, in our example we use four features: sky, temperature, humidity, and wind to make predictions about rain. These features would, however, be irrelevant for predicting, for example, the part of

TABLE 6.1 ● Examples of Occurrences for the Event "Rain"					
Instance	Sky	Temperature	Humidity	Wind	Rain?
1	Sunny	Warm	High	None	No
2	Overcast	Warm	High	Strong	Yes
3	Overcast	Cold	No	None	No
4	Overcast	Warm	High	Strong	Yes
5	Overcast	Cold	High	Strong	?

speech of a word, in which case we would use other features such as the word *before*, the word *after*, and so on. Event occurrences are typically represented as vectors of feature values, which represent an observation of a certain instance of that event. In the previously given example, one of the occurrences (instance number 1) has a value of "sunny" for the sky feature, a value of "high" for the humidity feature, and so forth. The event we are trying to predict is typically referred to as the "class." In our example, the class is rain, and it has two possible values: yes or no. Class values are known for the instances we are learning from (generally referred to as training instances) but are unknown for the instances we are trying to make predictions for (often referred to as test instances).

Given the feature vector representation of an event, along with specific instances of that event represented as vectors of feature and class values, there are many supervised learning algorithms that can be used. These algorithms are broadly classified into eager algorithms and lazy algorithms. Eager algorithms, which learn when presented with the training instances, build a model that can then be quickly applied to make predictions for test instances. Most supervised learning algorithms fall under this category. Examples of such algorithms are decision trees, neural networks, SVMs, Naive Bayes, and so forth. Lazy algorithms, which do not do any intensive work at training time, instead reserve most of the learning process for the time when the test instances become available. Nearest neighbor is an example of a lazy algorithm.

There are literally hundreds of applications of machine learning, which cannot possibly be listed all in one place. They range from weather prediction, as in the previously given example, to predictions of language phenomena (e.g., text classification, part of speech labeling, word sense predictions), to applications in psychology (e.g., prediction of psychological traits), sociology (e.g., prediction of communication patterns), astronomy (e.g., prediction of star presence or star moves), and so forth. As long as an application requires a prediction being made, and as long as there is some history of previously occurring examples where that prediction is known, machine learning can be applied to address the problem. While the amount of training data is an important aspect of any learning task, to some extent even more important is how the data is represented; in other words, what features are selected to describe the training and test instances? The following sections address feature representation and weighting and describe three supervised learning algorithms.

Feature Representation and Weighting

The features used to represent the instances of a learning problem can fall under two different types. They could be discrete features, taking values out of a finite set. For example, the value of the sky feature in the example shown in Table 6.1 can be either sunny or overcast. The values for a discrete feature do not have to be set a priori. Rather, it is typical to infer the set of values based on the training and test instances being observed. Features can also be continuous—that is, they take numerical values, which can be either integer or real values, positive or negative. It is also possible that the value of a feature is not observable for a certain instance, in which case it is explicitly marked as missing data to reflect the lack of information for that attribute for that instance.

Not all the features selected to describe a learning problem are equally useful. It is therefore important to have ways to measure the weight of each feature. This is generally done automatically by the learning algorithms themselves, which sift through the training instances and calculate how discriminatory each feature is (in other words, how much that feature helps in finding the right class for an instance).

Importantly, the weights associated with features are also a way to analyze and interpret a classification data set. Consider, for example, the problem of classifying the gender of the author of a text. It is, of course, useful to be able to say that a supervised learning algorithm—for example, a decision tree—can separate the two classes with an accuracy of 75%. But it is even more useful to be able to say that certain features—for example, the frequency of certain pronouns or other patterns in the data—are the ones that contribute most toward this classification, which can lead to insights into the differences between the two genders.

Feature Weighting

There are different weighting metrics that can be used to weight features. One of the most commonly used measures is information gain. Although the calculation of information gain is an integral part of most learning algorithms, we briefly describe it here, as it is simple to understand and can be used as a tool for data analysis.

Given a collection S of positive and negative instance, let p be the probability of an instance to be positive, and q the probability of an instance to be negative. We define its entropy as Entropy(S) = $-$ p log p $-$ q log q. The entropy is at its maximum when p = q = 1/2, and at its minimum when p = 1 and q = 0 (we use the assumption that log 0 = 0). For instance, if S contains 14 examples: 9 positive and 5 negative, Entropy(S) = $-$ (9/14) log (9/14) $-$ (5/14) log (5/14) = 0.94.

We can now define information gain as the expected reduction in entropy when we split a data set S based on a certain feature A.

$$Gain(S,A) = Entropy(S) - \sum_{v \in Values(A)} \frac{|S_v|}{|S|} Entropy(S_v)$$

Figure 6.1 shows an example of how information gain is calculated for two binary features. In this example, we have the problem of classifying a text, represented as a set of words, as either computer science (labeled as C) or biology (labeled as B). We assume a set of 14 training instances, consisting of 9 instances that belong to the class C, and 5 that belong to the class B. We have two features under consideration: one feature, named computer, with values yes or no (depending on whether the word *computer* is present in an instance), and a second feature named cell, again with values yes or no. We can then calculate the entropy of this data set before we split the data based on either of these two features; as before: Entropy(S) = $-$ (9/14) log (9/14) $-$ (5/14) log (5/14) = 0.94. We can also calculate the entropy of the data after following each of the branches for a certain feature. For example, if we follow the branch yes for the feature computer, meaning that we look only at those instances where this feature has a value of yes, we will find three instances in class C and 4 in class B, which corresponds to an entropy of Entropy($S_{Computer = yes}$) = $-$ (3/7) log (3/7) $-$ (4/7) log (4/7) = 0.985. Similarly, if we follow the branch no for the same feature, the entropy of the resulting set will be Entropy($S_{Computer = no}$) = 0.592. We can now combine all of these entropy values to calculate the information gain, by weighting each of the entropies corresponding to branches of the feature computer. There are 7 instances that fall under the branch yes for the feature computer, and thus, Entropy($S_{Computer = yes}$) will be weighted as 7/14. Just as a coincidence in this example, the entropy corresponding to the other branch will also have a weight of 7/14. After all the calculations are complete, we will conclude that between the two features considered, computer has a higher discriminatory power for this specific classification problem (with a information gain of 0.151, as compared to the information gain of cell, which is 0.048).

Supervised Learning Algorithms

There is a very large number of supervised learning algorithms that have been proposed to date—many of which have one or more publicly available implementations as stand-alone code or part of machine learning packages. Some of the most popular supervised learning algorithms are Naive Bayes (covered in detail in Chapter 11),

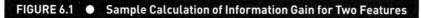

FIGURE 6.1 ● Sample Calculation of Information Gain for Two Features

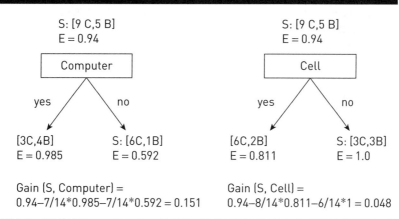

S: [9 C,5 B]
E = 0.94

Computer

yes   no

[3C,4B]   S: [6C,1B]
E = 0.985   E = 0.592

Gain (S, Computer) =
0.94−7/14*0.985−7/14*0.592 = 0.151

S: [9 C,5 B]
E = 0.94

Cell

yes   no

[6C,2B]   S: [3C,3B]
E = 0.811   E = 1.0

Gain (S, Cell) =
0.94−8/14*0.811−6/14*1 = 0.048

decision trees, instance based learning, SVMs (these three algorithms are covered below), linear regression, perceptrons and neural networks, and random forests.

Decision Trees

Decision tree learning (Quinlan, 1993) is one of many algorithms for eager learning, where a decision tree is built during the training stage and later used for making classification decisions on test instances. A decision tree is a structure that looks like a flowchart, where each internal node represents a test on one of the features, and the nodes represent classification decisions. For instance, Figure 6.2 shows one possible decision tree for the weather problem with the features shown in Table 6.1.

FIGURE 6.2 ● Sample Decision Tree Using Features Shown in Table 6.1

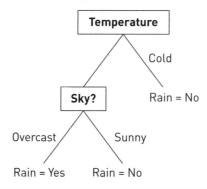

Temperature

Cold

Sky?   Rain = No

Overcast   Sunny

Rain = Yes   Rain = No

As with any eager learner, in a decision tree learning process, most of the time is spent in training, when the decision tree is built. There are a very large number of different decision trees that can be put together for one data set. In Figure 6.2, we show one possible decision tree for the features in Table 6.1; one could also imagine a tree that has *sky* at the root, or *humidity,* and then branches that use the other available features. As it turns out, the selection of features for inclusion in the decision tree can have an impact both in terms of effectiveness (how correct are the classifications made with a decision tree?) as well as in terms of efficiency (how fast can such classifications be made at test time?).

The typical process for building a decision tree is to iteratively select features based on their weight. Using information gain as a feature weighting measure (other weighting metrics can also be used), the most informative feature is selected from among all the features available and added as the root of the decision tree. Next, for each of the possible values of the feature selected as root, we determine the set of instances that have that feature value and once again determine the most informative feature from among the remaining features, with the information gain being measured on that set of instances. A branch is stopped when we reach a decision leaf, which is the case when we have one or multiple instances under a branch that have the same classification decision.

For example, if we choose temperature as the most informative feature for the instances in Table 6.1 and we include it as the root of the tree, we will first consider its warm value and determine the most informative feature on the set of instances 1, 2, and 4, from among the features sky, humidity, and wind; then repeat the same process for its cold value, and in this case, we will have reached a decision node, as we have a consensus over the classification for all the instances in this set (there is only one instance with a temperature value of cold, and we can thus make a decision when we notice this value). Assume we find sky to be the next most informative feature, we then apply the same process for each of its values, and so on.

Sometime decision trees can grow overly large, in which case the process of "pruning" can be applied, with the goal of reducing the complexity of the tree while keeping the accuracy of the classifier. There are different pruning techniques, one of the simplest being to replace each node with its most popular (frequent) class and keep the replacement if it does not affect the prediction accuracy.

Instance-Based Learning

Instance-based learning is a form of lazy learning and includes algorithms such as k-nearest neighbors (or kNN, for short) and kernel machines. The main idea underlying instance-based learning in general and kNN in particular is that a test instance can be classified by finding the most similar training instances and using their class as a label. Consider, for instance, the example shown in Figure 6.3, in which we want to classify the point labeled with a question mark as either a rectangle or a circle. A kNN algorithm will try to find the kNN and find the majority class among those

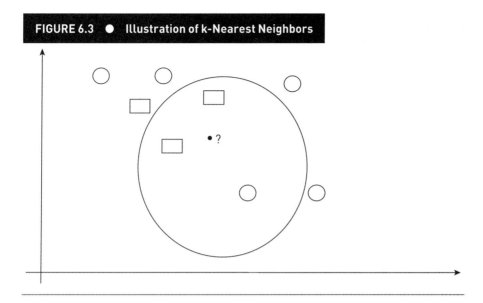

FIGURE 6.3 ● Illustration of k-Nearest Neighbors

instances. In this example, if we select the three-nearest neighbors, as shown inside the circle, the label will be dictated by the rectangle training instances, which are a majority.

Depending on the number of neighbors being considered, a different class may be assigned. For instance, in Figure 6.3, we could also apply a seven-nearest neighbors, in which case the label will be a circle.

A central issue for these algorithms is the measure of distance being used to decide which are the closest training instances for a given test instance. It is common to use a Euclidian distance, but other distance metrics can also be used. Considering the vector representations discussed previously and assuming a training vector X and a test vector Y, the Euclidian distance will be given by $\sqrt{\Sigma(x_i - y_i)^2}$. In recent years, various kernel measures have been often used, where a kernel is simply a similarity measure defined over a certain set of inputs (e.g., there are string kernels, which define the similarity of two strings and tree kernels, which measure the similarity of tree structures).

Support Vector Machines

The underlying idea behind SVM algorithms (Vapnik, 1995) is to identify a hyperplane (or set of hyperplanes) that can provide the best separation between the training data instances. Among all possible separation hyperplanes, SVM algorithms try to identify the one that has the largest distance to the nearest training instance of any class, as that will be reflected into a lower generalization error of the classifier.

Consider, for instance, the task of separating the rectangle and circle instances shown in Figure 6.4. Multiple hyperplanes can be drawn, including H_1, which does

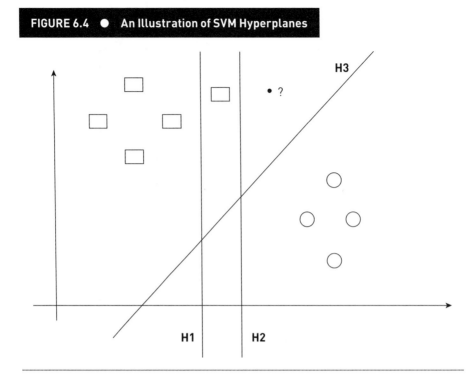

FIGURE 6.4 ● An Illustration of SVM Hyperplanes

not separate the two classes well; H_2, which separates the rectangles and circles, but with a small margin, as it is very close to a rectangle instance; and H_3, which again separates the instances in the two classes, with a larger margin. We will eventually choose this separation hyperplane and consequently determine the class of a new unknown item depending on where it falls with respect to this hyperplane. For example, the instance marked with a question mark in Figure 6.4 will be labeled as a rectangle, as it falls on the side of the selected hyperplane H_3 that belongs to the rectangle instances.

Given the feature vector representations discussed previously, in the feature space X, any hyperplane can be written as w.X – b = y. We then want to find the vector of weights w and parameter b so that the hyperplane separates all the instances in the training data with the largest margin. This is a quadratic optimization problem, which can be solved by using Lagrangian multiplier methods.

Note that SVM algorithms were devised to solve binary classification problems— that is, separate between instances belonging to two classes. However, any multiclass classification can be translated into a set of binary classifications, by performing multiple classifications of one versus all. Assume, for instance, we have three classes: A, B, and C. We can thus perform three binary classifications: A vs. (B or C); B vs. (A or C); and C vs. (A or B).

Evaluation of Supervised Learning

As with any automatic systems, it is important to have ways to evaluate supervised learning systems. Usually this is done on test data that is independent from the training data, using metrics such as accuracy, precision, or recall. Accuracy is defined as the total number of test instances that are correctly classified out of the total number of test instances. Precision and recall are defined with respect to one given class, C_i, the precision being the total number of instances correctly labeled as C_i by the system out of the total number of instances labeled as C_i by the system and recall being the total number of instances correctly labeled as C_i by the system out of the total number of instances labeled as C_i in the entire test data.

For more robust results, experiments are generally run over multiple training/test data splits, and the results obtained for different splits are averaged. That is, given a set of labeled instances, say 1,000, we could take 90% of this set and use it for training and the remaining 10% for test, then divide the 1,000 instances in another 90% to 10% split and repeat the evaluation, and so on. This also leads to N-fold cross-validation evaluations, when the set of labeled instances is split into N subsets, then one subset is used for test and the remaining N-1 subsets are used for training, then another subset is used for test and the remaining N-1 subsets for training, and so on N times, followed by an average over the set of N results. An alternative to that is leave-one-out cross-validation, where the test set consists of one single instance, and the training set consists of the remaining instances; this process again is repeated several times, for each instance in the data set.

Finally, very relevant for the evaluation of any classification system is its learning curve: How is the performance of the classifier affected by the size of the training data? To generate this curve, one can run the classification system on fractions of the training data and determine its accuracy on the same test set. Figure 6.5 shows two sample learning curves, with accuracies measured for two classifiers on fractions of training data ranging from 10% to 100%. Learning curves can be very insightful, as they can determine the course of future experiments: Should one focus on gathering more data (see the learning curve in Figure 6.5a, where the curve has an ascending trend), or is the data sufficient, and one should focus on engineering more sophisticated features (see the learning curve in Figure 6.5b, where the curve has plateaued after a certain number of training instances)?

Software for Supervised Learning

There are several extensive packages that cover a large number of supervised learning algorithms, including the following: Weka (http://www.cs.waikato.ac.nz/ml/weka), which is a Java toolkit with implementations of many machine learning algorithms, primarily geared toward data mining; Scikit (http://scikit-learn.org), a large Python library of machine learning tools; Caret (http://cran.r-project.org/web/packages/caret/

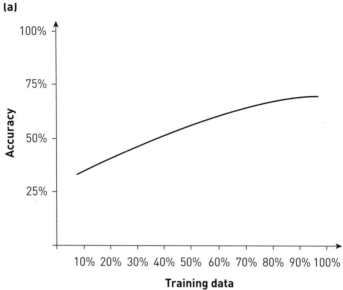

Figure 6.5 ● Learning Curves for Two Classifiers/Data Sets

(a)

(b)

index.html), and R package, including tools for data preprocessing, feature selection, and machine learning. There are also many implementations available for specific algorithms, including SVM[light] (http://svmlight.joachims.org) and Algorithm-DecisionTree (http://search.cpan.org/~avikak/Algorithm-DecisionTree-1.41).

Text Analysis Methods From the Humanities and Social Sciences

I n the three chapters in Part III, we selectively review text analysis techniques that have been developed primarily within the humanities and social sciences. The three techniques we cover—thematic analysis, narrative analysis, and metaphor analysis—can be considered forms of content analysis as outlined in the Approaches to Research Design section of Chapter 2. We chose to focus on these three particular approaches to text/content analysis because they are all at least potentially "mixed" methods that incorporate both quantitative and qualitative elements, and as such, they can be used with the web scraping and crawling methods reviewed in Part II as well as the text mining methods reviewed in Part IV. As we will see in the three chapters in Part III, researchers working in collaborative interdisciplinary teams are currently developing new ways of performing thematic analysis, narrative analysis, and metaphor analysis that take advantage of big data and Internet-related technology.

7

Thematic Analysis, Qualitative Data Analysis Software, and Visualization

Learning Objectives

The goals of Chapter 7 are to help readers do the following:

1. Learn thematic analysis as a qualitative method compatible with many different theoretical approaches to text analysis.

2. Become familiar with qualitative data analysis software (QDAS) used for thematic analysis (and for other text analysis approaches as well).

3. Learn about software tools for visualizing texts' themes and their interrelations in text corpora.

Thematic Analysis

Thematic analysis is a method for identifying, analyzing, and reporting patterns of themes within text corpora. At a minimum, it involves organizing and describing texts in detail but can go further than organization and description by allowing for interpretation of various aspects of the research topic (Boyatzis, 1998). While thematic analysis is widely used in the social sciences, there is little clear agreement about how best to go about doing it. Braun and Clarke (2006) have suggested that it is a poorly "branded" method that is not widely viewed as a "named" analysis in contrast to more widely recognized approaches such as narrative analysis (see Chapter 8). But thematic analysis is arguably a foundational method for qualitative approaches to text analysis, as it provides core skills that are useful for conducting many different forms of text analysis. For this reason, Boyatzis (1998) characterized thematic analysis not as a specific method but as a tool to use across different methods and theoretical approaches, and Ryan and Bernard (2000) located thematic coding as a process compatible with major analytic traditions rather than a specific methodological approach in its own right (also see Ryan & Bernard, 2010, p. 53; cf. Braun & Clarke, 2006). Because thematic analysis is performed within many analytic traditions, it can be used to do many different things, and as such, its results depend critically on researchers' theoretical positions and values.

Thematic analysis starts when the researcher notices patterns of meaning in a collection of texts—either during the process of acquiring texts or soon after. The end point is the reporting of the content and meaning of the patterns of themes in the corpus. While thematic analysis allows researchers to interpret overarching themes and subthemes in texts, it does not allow them to make claims about language use or the "fine-grained functionality of talk" (Braun & Clarke, 2006, p. 28). Still, themes are understood to capture something important about the data in relation to the research question. An important question to address in terms of coding is what counts as a theme. This is a question of prevalence both in terms of the frequency of the occurrence of a theme within each text as well as across the entire corpus. While ideally there will be a number of instances of the theme within the corpus, more instances do not necessarily mean the theme itself is more crucial, and there are as of yet no agreed upon answers to the question of what proportion of a corpus needs to display evidence of a theme for it to be considered a main or overarching theme. The "keyness" of a theme is thus not necessarily based on quantifiable measures but rather on whether it captures something important in relation to the overall research question (Braun & Clarke, 2006).

In thematic analysis, themes can be identified either inductively or deductively (see Chapter 7). A "bottom-up" inductive approach means that the themes identified are directly linked to the texts being analyzed (Patton, 1990). In this approach, if the corpus has been constructed specifically for the research (e.g., by transcribing interviews or focus group interactions), the themes identified may bear little relationship to the specific questions that were asked of the participants (see, e.g., Toerien & Wilkinson, 2004). In contrast, "top-down" deductive thematic analysis is driven by the researcher's theoretical or substantive questions.

Distinct from most text analysis and text mining methods, in thematic analysis writing is an integral part of every phase of a research project. Writing generally begins in a project's initial stages with the writing out of ideas and potential coding schemes and continues through coding and analysis phases. Because thematic analysis is not a linear process but rather a recursive one where the analyst moves back and forth as needed throughout a project's many phases, the first steps in a thematic analysis are for the researcher to acquire a collection of texts and to immerse herself in the corpus via "repeated reading" (Braun & Clarke, 2006). Such immersion and repeated reading involves searching for themes while reading the texts carefully and taking extensive notes.

Formal coding starts with the researcher generating initial codes based on the notes taken while actively and repeatedly reading the texts. Codes identify a feature of the corpus that is interesting to the researcher and refer to "the most basic segment, or element, of the raw data or information that can be assessed in a meaningful way regarding the phenomenon" (Boyatzis 1998, p. 63). Coding can be done either manually or with specialized software (see the next section of this chapter). If coding manually, analysts can write notes on the texts themselves, using highlighters or colored pens to indicate potential patterns, or on sticky notes. But coded data differs from the units of analysis, which are themes developed in the next phase of the analysis.

The next phase of thematic analysis begins when all texts have been initially coded and the researcher has a list of different codes identified in the corpus. At this point, the researcher refocuses on themes rather than codes: The different codes are sorted into potential themes, and coded data extracts are collated within the identified themes. In this phase, the researcher may use visual representations such as matrices or mind maps (see the Visualization Tools section) to help sort codes into themes and may also begin to consider the relationships between different levels of themes, such as between overarching themes and subthemes, and to review, revise, and organize themes and possibly recode data based on the revised set of themes. The goal is for words and concepts associated with themes to cohere together meaningfully while there are clear and identifiable distinctions between themes (Patton, 2014).

Researchers have several observational techniques available to sort coded text into themes. One technique is to identify themes by recognizing repetitions in coded text. For example, Strauss (1992) analyzed interviews with a retired blue-collar worker and found that he repeatedly referred to ideas associated with money, businessmen, greed, siblings, and "being different" and concluded that these ideas represented important themes in his life. Researchers may also notice local terms that are used in unfamiliar ways. Such "indigenous categories" (Patton, 1990) can provide insights into the typologies and classification schemes of the community being investigated. Well-known examples of studies of indigenous classifications are Spradley's (1972) analysis of tramps' typology of different types of "flops" (places to sleep) and Becker's (1993) analysis of medical students' indigenous category of "crock." As is discussed in detail in Chapter 9, another way for researchers to identify themes in texts is by focusing on metaphorical language. Researchers can also analyze transitions, or "naturally occurring shifts in content" (Ryan & Bernard, 2003, p. 90) that may take the form of pauses or particular phrases (see Silverman, 1993, pp. 114–143).

Jones, Coviello, and Tang's (2011) study of academic research on international entrepreneurship is an example of inductive thematic analysis. Jones and colleagues (2011) constructed a corpus from 323 journal articles on international entrepreneurship published between 1989 and 2009 and inductively synthesized and categorized themes and subthemes in their data. Another example of inductive thematic analysis is Toerien and Wilkinson's (2004) study of women's body hair removal. Toerien and Wilkinson (2004) analyzed responses to open-ended questions from a survey of 678 women in the United Kingdom, and their thematic analysis revealed depilation to be a matter not merely of personal preference but of conforming to social norms reflecting an imperative to improve the body.

Frith and Gleeson's (2004) study of male body image is a more theoretically driven thematic analysis. In order to better understand how men's feelings about their bodies influence their clothing practices, Frith and Gleeson (2004) used a snowball sampling strategy to recruit undergraduate psychology students who answered four written questions about clothing practices and body image. Thematic analysis of the students' answers revealed four main themes relevant to the research question (see Suerdem, 2010, for an attempt to bridge inductive and deductive approaches to thematic analysis).

Qualitative Data Analysis Software

Thematic analysis can be performed without the help of specialized software, but software can help to expand the scope, methodological sophistication, and rigor of thematic analysis projects. The most popular software used for thematic analysis is known as computer-assisted qualitative data analysis software (CAQDAS, or QDAS [qualitative data analysis software] for short). QDAS packages are tools for organizing collections of documents so that they can be more efficiently and effectively analyzed qualitatively, although several QDAS packages include modules for statistical analysis and data visualization (see the Visualization Tools section). Such software is widely used in psychology, marketing research, and ethnography and typically includes tools for searching for content; coding (or labeling) text; linking text units; querying; writing and annotation; and visualizing results as maps, networks, or word clouds (see the Visualization Tools section).

Versions of QDAS have been around since the 1980s and have been used to assist content analysis, discourse analysis, grounded theory analysis, and mixed method projects. The first version of the QDAS program NUD*IST was released in 1981, and ATLAS and WinMax in 1989. These software packages subsequently evolved into more developed forms: WinMax into MAXQDA, ATLAS into ATLAS.ti, and NUD*IST into NVivo.

QDAS packages perform several interrelated functions for researchers. First and foremost, they allow researchers to code and retrieve samples of text. They also allow researchers to use coded text to build theoretical models of the processes—be they social, psychological, cognitive, linguistic, or some combination of these—that are thought to have generated the text. Their interfaces also allow for relatively easy text retrieval and for management of and navigation within large document collections. In addition to these core functions, as we will see, many software packages allow for visualization and statistical analysis of the interrelationships between coded textual units.

A central feature of QDAS is the ability to set up rules to apply labels to texts. QDAS packages offer a variety of text coding techniques that allow for code and retrieve functionality, including *in vivo coding*, an inductive method where a word or short phrase taken from the text itself is the code or label (King, 2008). Other forms of coding include *free coding*, which involves assigning any code to arbitrary sequences of data; *contextual coding*, in which users label text in such a way as to allow them to quickly navigate to view the labeled text in context; *automatic coding*, which involves assigning codes automatically to search results; and even artificial intelligence–based *software-generated coding*, in which the software suggests codes based on its own analysis of the text.

QDAS packages feature a number of different types of text search tools, including simple searches; Boolean searches using the Boolean operators AND, OR, and NOT; placeholder searches that allow you to use placeholders for certain characters; and proximity searches that allow you to retrieve combinations of two or more text strings and/or codes that occur in a definable proximity to each other. Fuzzy searches, or "approximation searches," are exclusive to NVivo (as of this writing). These allow you to perform searches that retrieve textual data even if the data contains typographic errors. Combination searches involve combinations of some of the above types of searches.

In addition to coding and searching texts, QDAS packages provide a variety of different tools for annotation (e.g., memo writing and storage) and for producing output in different formats, from variable diagrams and network diagrams for visualizing theoretical models to word clouds. Most software allows users to export data on code and word frequencies to allows for statistical analysis with appropriate statistical packages such as SPSS or Stata, or else include statistical tools for analyzing word frequencies, cross-tabulations, clusters, and word co-occurrence matrices.

Research in psychology—and more recently in computational linguistics—has often made use of the Linguistic Inquiry and Word Count (LIWC) resource, described in Chapter 4, which maps words to psycholinguistic word categories that reflect properties such as *positive, certainty,* and others. Similarly, lexical resources such as *Roget's Thesaurus* or WordNet-Affect, also described in Chapter 4, group words into word classes. Text classification, covered in detail in Chapter 11, can sometimes be used to classify text into such themes. When the goal, however, is to *understand the characteristics* of a certain type of text, in order to gain a better understanding of the properties or behaviors modeled by those texts (such as *happiness, humor,* or *gender*), then the systematic identification of broad word classes characteristic to the given type of text is considerably more insightful than a figure reflecting the accuracy of a text classifier. One tool that can perform such modeling of text with respect to a predefined grouping of words into classes is linguistic ethnography (Mihalcea & Pulman, 2009), which, given a collection of texts characterized by a certain property, automatically discovers the classes that are dominant in those texts. Briefly, the method uses the normalized frequency of the words in the word classes inside the target collection of texts and compares that to the normalized frequency of those same words inside texts that do not share the same property. This ratio is used to calculate a dominance score for each word class, which can be used to determine the importance of that word class for the given collection of texts. For instance, for a collection of jokes Mihalcea and Pulman (2009) found that word classes that reflect *humans* (e.g., *wife, lawyer*) or *negativity* (e.g., *not, bad*) are dominant in humorous texts when compared to regular nonhumorous documents.

While QDAS packages are popular and widely used in several disciplines, it is important to note that the desirability of using software in qualitative analysis has been vigorously debated. Coffey, Holbrook, and Atkinson (1996); Macmillan (2005); and Goble, Austin, Larsen, Kreitzer, and Brintnell (2012) are good places to start for critical appraisals of QDAS, as is the debate on White, Judd, and Poliandri's paper "Illumination With a Dim Bulb?" published in the journal *Sociological Methodology* in 2012. While this latter debate is concerned specifically with computational narrative analysis methods (see Chapter 8), it covers some important issues that should be considered by any researcher interested in using QDAS.

The most widely used QDAS packages are described in Table 7.1. Although free trial versions of most of these are available, the full versions can be expensive—particularly for single users who do not have access to a group license.

So in addition to the packages in Table 7.1, researchers should be aware of the many free and open source QDAS tools that may meet their needs. Researchers who already use the programming language R or who are considering using it for quantitative analysis, can use the RQDA (R-based qualitative data analysis) package to combine text coding with the statistical power of R. RQDA is probably the most advanced of

TABLE 7.1 ● Qualitative Data Analysis Software Packages

Software	Description
ATLAS.ti	One of the first and most highly developed QDAS tools, it allows coded data to be exported for analysis with statistical packages such as SPSS. http://atlasti.com
Dedoose	A web-based qualitative and mixed methods research application, Dedoose builds on tools available in its predecessor, EthnoNotes. Dedoose is specifically designed to support the concurrent analysis of large amounts of mixed data by teams of geographically dispersed researchers. http://www.dedoose.com
f4analyse	f4analyse is a basic, easy-to-use, and competitively priced QDAS tool from Germany. http://www.audiotranskription.de/english/f4-analyse
HyperRESEARCH	HyperRESEARCH is QDAS for the Apple Mac OS. It features advanced multimedia capabilities. http://www.researchware.com/products/hyperresearch.html
Kwalitan	Designed to assist in the development of grounded theories, this software from the Netherlands enables hierarchical coding and the navigation of data with Boolean searches. http://www.kwalitan.nl
MAXQDA	A sophisticated package with statistical and visualization add-ons available. http://www.maxqda.com
NVivo	NVivo features relatively elaborate organizing functions that allow users to link together text data in a variety of ways. http://www.qsrinternational.com/products_nvivo.aspx
QDA Miner	QDA Miner is a sophisticated QDAS tool that integrates with SimStat, a statistical data analysis module, and WordStat, a quantitative content analysis and text mining module. http://provalisresearch.com/products/qualitative-data-analysis-software
Qualrus	Qualrus is a QDAS tool that is "portable" for use on multiple platforms (Mac, Windows). http://www.qualrus.com
Quirkos	Quirkos is an easy-to-use and competitively priced QDAS tool from the University of Edinburgh. http://www.quirkos.com/index.html

all the free QDAS packages. It allows users to perform word cloud analysis (see the Visualization Tools section), create queries for complex cross-coding retrieval, program auto-coding commands, plot the relationship between codes, and export data as spreadsheets, among other features. RQDA also features a very intuitive user interface.

TABLE 7.2 ● Free and Open Source Qualitative Data Analysis Software

Software	Description
AnSWR	Available from the U.S. Centers for Disease Control and Prevention, AnSWR is a software system for coordinating and conducting large-scale, team-based analysis projects that integrate qualitative and quantitative techniques. http://www.cdc.gov/hiv/library/software/answr/index.html
AQUAD	AQUAD is a German open source QDAS package with sophisticated features including Boolean search. http://www.aquad.de/en
Cassandre	Cassandre is a free QDAS package for Windows, Mac, and Linux from Belgium. Most documentation is in French. http://www.cassandre.ulg.ac.be
Coding Analysis Toolkit (or CAT)	CAT is a free web-based tool—originally from the University of Pittsburgh and the University of Massachusetts Amherst. CAT was designed to use mainly keystrokes rather than the mouse for coding and can import an ATLAS.ti project for quantitative analysis, though it has a coding mechanism built into itself as well. http://cat.textifer.com
CATMA	CATMA is software for Windows, Mac, OS ,and Linux developed at the University of Hamburg mainly for humanities researchers. http://catma.de
Compendium	Compendium is a general-purpose sharing and collaboration tool from the Open University in the United Kingdom. http://compendium.open.ac.uk/institute
FreeQDA	FreeQDA is an open source QDAS tool. http://freeqda.sourceforge.net
libreQDA	libreQDA is a free Spanish-language QDAS tool from Uruguay. http://www.libreqda.edu.uy
Linguistic Ethnography	Linguistic Ethnography is a free Perl package that determines the word classes that are dominant in a collection of texts. http://web.eecs.umich.edu/~mihalcea/downloads.html#LingEthn
Open Code	Free from Umea University in Sweden, Open Code was originally developed for use with grounded theory but now is a general-purpose qualitative data analysis tool. http://www.phmed.umu.se/english/units/epidemiology/research/open-code

(Continued)

TABLE 7.2 ● (Continued)

Software	Description
QDA Miner Lite	This is an easy-to-use version of QDA Miner that offers basic QDAS features. http://provalisresearch.com/products/qualitative-data-analysis-software/freeware
RQDA	RQDA is a package for the popular programming language R. Used with R, it performs both qualitative and quantitative analysis. http://rqda.r-forge.r-project.org
Saturate	Saturate is an online QDAS tool from the University of Huddersfield in the United Kingdom. http://onlineqda.hud.ac.uk/Step_by_step_software/Saturate
TAMS	An open source QDAS tool, TAMS is short for Text Analysis Markup System. http://sourceforge.net/projects/tamsys
TAMS Analyzer	TAMS Analyzer works with TAMS to allow users to efficiently assign codes to text passages. http://tamsys.sourceforge.net

Beyond RQDA, there are dozens of free and open source tools available, including QDA Miner Lite, which is a free version of QDA Miner with limited features for both PC and Mac, Open Code (PC only), Saturate (cloud), and CAT (cloud). Some of these packages are quite sophisticated: TAMS, AnSWR, and RQDA allow both inductive and deductive coding as well as coding memos, can support hierarchical or structured coding, provide basic coding statistics, and perform text and coding retrieval. For quick and simple coding, Open Code and Saturate are easy to use, although they allow only one code per predefined text segment. Saturate is particularly well suited for coding with more than one analyst.

Different types of research projects require QDAS packages with different sets of features. Some QDAS packages feature dashboards that are especially easy to use, others have more powerful project management and data organization tools, while still others allow users to easily explore and interact with their data. See Table 7.3.

Although social scientists may be tempted to use the software that is most readily available to them, it is worth investing some time in carefully calculating the benefits and disadvantages of the various software tools that might be used for a given project. Because the learning curve for some of these packages is steep and the time commitment involved substantial, it is important to choose the best tool for the job. That being said, Loughborough University's QDAS site provides some useful guidelines for matching software to research project requirements. They recommend MAXQDA

TABLE 7.3 ● QDAS Tips
Different packages are best suited to different types of research projects. Don't rush when selecting a package.
Check that the package you select can output codes in formats you can use at later stages of your research—for example, for statistical analysis or visualization.
Explore the QDAS comparison site at Loughborough University: http://www.restore.ac.uk/lboro/research/software/QDAS_comparison.php
Explore the site of the CAQDAS Networking Project: http://www.surrey.ac.uk/sociology/research/researchcentres/caqdas

or QDA Miner for mixed methods projects; NVivo and ATLAS.ti for discourse analysis (see Chapter 2); and ATLAS.ti, HyperRESEARCH, or Qualrus for virtual ethnography. It is, of course, important to refer to the software sites to keep up to date on new features, as new versions of both commercial and open source software are released frequently.

Visualization Tools

Software tools for visualization of patterns of word use and themes in texts are increasingly popular in the social sciences. Such tools have proven their value both in helping researchers to identify patterns in complex data and in presenting results of their studies in convenient visual formats. In this section, we survey visualization tools that can be used with QDAS packages as well as in combination with other types of software, for thematic analysis as well as for narrative analysis (Chapter 8), metaphor analysis (Chapter 9), and other approaches to text analysis.

While the field of visualization is developing rapidly and new tools for visualizing themes and other patterns in texts are introduced regularly, these tools have some limitations that should be kept in mind at every stage of a research project. The majority of visualization techniques ultimately transform qualitative data into quantifiable segments, an approach to analysis that may be antithetical to the goals of qualitative research methods (see Biernacki, 2014). If done poorly, visualizations may distract from the meaning and power of text rather than add insight. Visual transformation of texts may result in a loss of emotional tone and nuances of meaning and may also lead to the impression that an analysis is less ambiguous and contradictory than it actually is. Thus, social scientists who are not convinced that visualization demonstrably improves the clarity and utility of their analyses and findings should consider relying on text excerpts or longer narratives to explore their texts and communicate their findings to their audiences.

There are many software tools available to visually represent words and themes in texts (see Henderson & Segal, 2013), including advanced tools such as correspondence analysis (LeRoux & Rouanet, 2010), path and network diagrams (Durland & Fredericks, 2005), decision trees (Ryan & Bernard, 2010), and sentiment analysis (Gregory et al., 2006). In the remainder of this chapter, we survey several of the most accessible visualization tools for text analysis including word clouds, word trees and phrase nets, matrices and maps, and key words in context.

Word Clouds

Word clouds provide a visual display of word counts from one or more texts. The more frequently a word appears, the larger the word is displayed in a word cloud visual (Viégas & Wattenberg, 2008). It has been only relatively recently that word counts have become easy to display visually in word or tag clouds through popular online applications such as Wordle (www.wordle.net) or TagCrowd (www.tagcrowd .com), and word cloud tools have been added to many QDAS packages including NVivo, ATLAS.ti, Dedoose, and MAXQDA (see the Qualitative Data Analysis Software section). Although word cloud software creates dramatic visuals, significant concerns have been brought up about its use. One concern is that word clouds rely entirely on word frequency and do not provide context for readers to understand how words are used within a text (Harris, 2011). Word clouds are unable to differentiate between words with positive or negative connotations, and they can be visually misleading because longer words take more space within the cloud (Viégas & Wattenberg, 2008, p. 51). Despite these concerns, word clouds' ease of use can make them a practical tool for social scientists if they are used sparingly and their limitations are acknowledged. Although not very useful for complex analysis, they can be used in a project's early phases to help researchers identify keywords in texts or compare multiple corpora or documents (Weisgerber & Butler, 2009). For example, two or more word clouds can be shown together to contrast word usage across corpora or documents. Advanced word cloud visualizations such as parallel tag clouds (Collins, Viégas, & Wattenberg, 2009) and spark clouds (Lee, Riche, Karlson, & Carpendale, 2010) are recent developments that allow users to compare multiple word clouds. Finally, when coupled with written analysis and explanation, word clouds can be used to illustrate ideas or themes for lay audiences.

Word Trees and Phrase Nets

The two main tools for visualizing texts in terms of sentences and short phrases (rather than single words as in word clouds) are word trees and phrase nets. These tools were originally developed as part of the IBM project Many Eyes (http://www-01.ibm .com/software/analytics/many-eyes) but are now available in NVivo and other QDAS packages. Word tree software allows researchers to see how a particular word is used in sentences or phrases and provides visual displays of the connection of an identified word or words to other words in a corpus through a branching system (Wattenberg

& Viégas, 2008). These systems allow the researcher to have the tree branch to words that come either before or after the identified word, providing some context for words, which is an improvement over word clouds. For example, Henderson and Segal (2013) examined the relationship between a research university and local community organizations and found that the understandings and goals of research varied for the two groups. A word tree created from the study's documents displayed all of the sentences that contain the word *research* to provide a better understanding of how this word was used and the variation of its use. Although they resemble word trees, phrase nets differ from word trees in that they focus on connections of word pairs rather than whole sentences (see van Ham, Wattenberg, & Viégas, 2009).

Although sentence visualization tools provide more contextual information than single word analysis, they are best suited for exploratory data analysis (Weisgerber & Butler, 2009) rather than for complex analysis or hypothesis testing. By focusing on key words within sentences, word trees and phrase maps allow social scientists to quickly identify patterns of word use within corpora and whether words are being used in divergent ways within or across texts.

Matrices and Maps

Matrices and maps are tools for the visualization of themes (rather than words or sentences) in texts. Since the process of identifying themes requires at least an initial analysis of the texts (see the Thematic Analysis section of this chapter), visualization of themes is more valuable in the analysis and reporting phases of a project than in exploratory phases. Because researchers can rank themes or place them into nonordinal categories, visualizing a corpus at the thematic level offers more options and dimensions for visual representations than at the word or sentence level.

Matrices are sets of numbers arranged in rows or columns. In text analysis, a matrix involves "the crossing of two or more dimensions . . . to see how they interact" (Miles & Huberman, 1994, p. 239). Matrices are very useful for organizing textual data (see Chapter 2) and for visualizing the relationships between and among categories of data, examining how categories relate to theoretical concepts, and searching for propositions linking categories of data. Similar to a cluster heat map (Wilkinson & Friendly, 2009) or an ethnoarray (Dohan, Abramson, & Miller, 2012), a benefit of matrices is that they provide an overview of thematic patterns within corpora and allow for comparison between corpora. As with QDAS packages' increased capabilities with word clouds, most qualitative software packages have the ability to create a matrix based on theme frequency with links to the corresponding text within the program. However, because matrices do not provide the stories or context behind the themes they organize, ideally, when creating matrices or other visualizations, researchers should link the individual boxes to quotes that support reader understanding of the theme.

Like matrices, mind maps and concept maps (Trochim, 1989; Wheeldon & Ahlberg, 2012) focus on the connections and relations between themes. In mind maps and concept maps, arrows indicate the direction of influence and can be made different thicknesses to signify the degree of connection if that information is available. Maps can be easily created for data analysis and reporting with standard or specialized software such as ATLAS.ti, MAXQDA, and NVivo. For example Trochim, Cook, and Setze (1994) used concept mapping to develop a conceptual framework of the views of 14 staff members of a psychiatric rehabilitation agency's views of a program of supported employment for individuals with severe mental illness. And Wheeldon and Faubert (2009) showed how concept maps can be used in data collection in an exploratory study of the perceptions of four Canadians.

Key Word in Context

Several related visualization tools are based on word-counting techniques. These tools tell researchers which words occur most frequently and in what contexts within a corpus. Key word in context (KWIC) tools are modern versions of concordances (see Chapter 1) that list every substantive word in a text along with the words that surround them—for example, five words to the left and/or right. Ryan and Bernard (2010, p. 192) demonstrated the value of KWIC by analyzing the different ways the word *deconstruction* is used within academic texts. Software packages such as WordSmith include KWIC tools.

Software for Thematic Analysis, Qualitative Data Analysis, and Visualization

This chapter has focused on software for qualitative data analysis and data visualization, and links to software tools are provided throughout the chapter (see, especially, Tables 7.1 and 7.2).

8

Narrative Analysis

● ┌───

Learning Objectives

The goals of Chapter 8 are to help readers do the following:

1. Learn the major theoretical approaches to the analysis of narrative.

2. Learn qualitative, mixed, and quantitative narrative text analysis techniques.

3. Gain an awareness of the strengths and limitations of, and debates over, narrative analysis research methods.

4. Gain familiarity with specialized software used for narrative analysis.

I n this chapter, we review text analysis techniques based on narrative. Narrative analysis methods are used in anthropology, sociology, literary studies, and other fields to analyze how people come to interpret their social worlds and the events and actors in them and how they develop social identities through stories they tell about themselves and others. Narrative analysis first emerged as a discipline in the early 20th century, and spurred by the post–1960s qualitative movement in the social sciences, interest in the field surged in the late 20th century. Other factors contributing to the renewed interest in narrative included the "memoir boom" in literature and popular culture (Smith & Watson, 2010) and the turn to explorations of personal life in therapies of various kinds (Illouz, 2008).

Today, narrative analysis refers to a family of approaches in the humanities and social sciences to texts that take a narrative form. Narrative analysts study all sorts of texts, from interview transcripts to newspaper articles, speeches, plays, and works of literature. The main elements that give such texts narrative form are *sequences* and *consequences* of events by which narratives organize, connect, and evaluate events as meaningful for particular audiences. With these elements, storytellers interpret the social world and experience for their audiences.

We begin this chapter with a brief overview of major schools of thought in narrative analysis and then review exemplary studies that use qualitative and mixed methods of narrative analysis, focusing on these studies' research designs and methodologies. The chapter ends with a brief survey of specialized software that has been developed for narrative analysis.

Conceptual Foundations

Narrative analysis focuses on the ways people make and use stories to interpret the world. Narrative analysis does not treat narratives as stories that transmit a set of facts about the world and so is not primarily interested in whether stories are true or not. Narrative researchers view narratives as social products that are produced by people in specific social, historical, and cultural contexts. Narratives are understood to be interpretive devices through which people represent themselves and their worlds to themselves and others. Narratologists argue that people's representations of themselves often take narrative forms and that "public stories" circulating in popular culture provide resources people use both to construct their personal narratives and identities (Ricoeur, 1991) and to link the present to the past. Such stories are often found in interview accounts (Gee, 1991).

Narratives are characterized by *transformation* (change over time) of *actions* and *characters* that are brought together in a *plot line*. Stories bring together many plot elements, including digressions and subplots, in what is known as a process of "emplotment" (White, 1978). Narratives must have a point, which often takes the form of a moral message.

Although scholars in diverse disciplines have developed many different methods for analyzing narratives, three of the most influential approaches are *structural, functional,* and *sociological* approaches.

Structural Approaches to Narrative

Structural approaches to narrative analysis operate mainly at a *textual* level of analysis rather than at *contextual* or *sociological* levels (see Chapter 2). The focus of structural narrative analysis is what is known as a "story grammar." An early theorist of story grammars, Propp (1968) argued that the fairytale has a narrative form that is central to all storytelling. The fairytale is structured not by the nature of the characters in it but by the function they play in the plot, and the number of possible functions is fairly small. In his influential structural approach to narrative, Labov (1972) defined narrative as "one method of recapitulating past experience by matching a verbal sequence of clauses to the sequence of events which (it is inferred) actually occurred" (pp. 359–360; see also Labov & Waletzky, 1967, p. 20). For Labov (1972), a "minimal narrative" is "a sequence of two clauses which are temporally ordered." The skeleton of a narrative thus consists of a series of temporally ordered clauses called "narrative clauses" (pp. 360–361). While narratives require narrative clauses, not all clauses found in narrative are narrative clauses. Labov (1972) provided the following example:

    A. I know a boy named Harry.
    B. Another boy threw a bottle at him right in the head.
    C. He got seven stitches.

In this narrative passage, only clauses B and C are narrative clauses. Clause A is a "free clause" in Labov's (1972) terminology because it does not have a temporal component. It can be moved freely within the text without altering the text's meaning. This is not so with narrative clauses, where a rearrangement of the clauses typically results in a change in meaning (p. 360). Labov also proposed that there are six distinct functional parts in a fully formed narrative: the (1) abstract, (2) orientation, (3) complicating action, (4) evaluation, (5) result or resolution, and (6) coda. Of these six parts, only the complicating action, which constitutes the main body of clauses and "usually comprises a series of events" (Labov & Waletzky, 1967, p. 32), is "essential if we are to recognize a narrative" (Labov, 1972, p. 370).

Functionalist Approaches to Narrative

Functionalist approaches to narrative operate at psychological and contextual levels of analysis rather than at purely textual or sociological levels (Chapter 2). The functional approach to narrative was pioneered by the psychologist Jerome Bruner (1990), who argued that humans' ordering of experience occurs in two modes. The first is the paradigmatic or *logico-scientific mode*, which attempts to fulfill the ideal of a formal, mathematical system of description and explanation. This mode is typical of argumentation in the physical sciences and philosophy. In contrast, in the *narrative mode* of ordering experience, it is events' particularity and specificity as well as people's involvement, accountability, and responsibility in bringing about specific events that are centrally important.

Functionalist analysis of narrative differs from structuralist analysis in that it focuses on what particular stories *do* in the contexts of people's everyday lives rather than the structural elements of texts themselves. For Bruner, the functions of narrative include mainly *solving problems*, *reducing tension*, and *resolving dilemmas*. Narratives allow people to deal with and explain mismatches between the exceptional and the ordinary. Narratives are not required when events occur that are perceived as ordinary but are needed to allow people to recast unfamiliar or chaotic experiences into causal stories in order to make sense of such experiences and to render them familiar and safe. Closely related to Bruner's approach are Lev Vygotsky's functionalist *social development theory* (Wertsch, 1985) and M. A. K. Halliday's (2006) *systemic functional grammar*, as well as Michael Bamberg's (2004) psychological research using functionalist narrative methods to investigate adolescent and postadolescent identity formation and the emergence of professional identities (see Chapter 2).

Functionalist approaches to narrative have influenced the "life story tradition" in narratology, psychology, and management research. Psychologists, for instance, have used autobiographical narratives both for research and in therapeutic practice. Their interest is not mainly in the content of life stories per se but in how individuals recount their histories: what they emphasize and omit, their stances as protagonists or victims, and the relationships their stories establish between teller and audience (see Rosenwald & Ochberg, 1992). For researchers in this tradition, personal stories are not only ways of telling someone (or oneself) about one's life but are means by which personal identities are fashioned.

Sociological Approaches to Narrative

Sociological approaches to narrative focus on the cultural, historical, and political contexts in which particular stories are, or can be, told by particular narrators to particular audiences. The British sociologist Ken Plummer's (1995) *Telling Sexual Stories* is one such sociological narrative analysis of "coming out stories," which Plummer argues are "rites of a sexual story-telling culture." This culture emerged in the late 20th century and involved the transformation of experiences once seen as personal, private, and pathological into public and political stories. Plummer's (1995) study of the proliferation of these types of narratives is based on transcribed interviews with people narrating their own biographical stories involving recovering from rape or coming out as gay or lesbian and of fashioning personal identities based on participation in communities based on common sexual identity or common political goals related to intimate experience.

Mixed Methods of Narrative Analysis

Most studies based on structuralist, functionalist, and sociological approaches to narrative use exclusively qualitative, interpretive methods. However, since the 1980s, sociologists, psychologists, and other social researchers have developed mixed methods that integrate interpretive methods into sophisticated research designs that allow for statistical analysis of patterns of words in narratives. For example, based on a structuralist theory of narrative, Sudhahar, Franzosi, and Cristianini (2011) have developed mixed methods for analyzing narrative grammars that attempt to quantify a basic structural element of what Bruner (1990) termed the *narrative mode* of ordering experience. For Franzosi, that element is a social cognitive process whereby people interpret situations of all kinds in terms of basic social relations of actors, actions, and objects of action. Franzosi's term for these sequential structures is the *semantic triplet* or *S-A-O triplet* (for *subject, action,* and *object*). His method of analyzing texts' semantic sequences involves teams of manual coders coding collections of historical texts, such as newspaper archives (1987), line-by-line for S-A-O triplets. Franzosi, De Fazio, and Vicari (2012) have applied this method in studies of newspaper accounts of lynchings and of the rise of fascism (see also Franzosi, 2010), while Cerulo (1998) has used it in her studies of "victim" and "perpetrator" sequences in newspaper headlines and Ignatow (2004) analyzed narrative grammars in a multimethod quantitative study of transcripts of shipyard union leaders' meetings (see Chapter 9).

The sociologist Roberts and his colleagues have developed another mixed method of narrative analysis that they term *modality analysis.* Similar in some ways to Franzosi's narrative grammars, the modality analysis is intended for cross-cultural and cross-linguistic comparative research (Roberts, 2008). Modality analysis evaluates languages by analyzing modal clauses in multiple large collections of text in multiple languages in order to identify what activities the users of each language treat as possible, impossible, inevitable, or contingent. Roberts and his colleagues have used their method to analyze the characteristics of many different cultures based on studies of Arab and Hindi newspapers (Roberts, Zuell, Landmann, & Wang, 2010) and Hungarian newspapers (Roberts, Popping, & Pan, 2009).

More recently, Mische (2014) has analyzed online documents from the UN Conference on Sustainable Development and the accompanying People's Summit held in Rio de Janeiro in 2012. Reading the documents, Mische and her team of graduate students noticed that the different groups who participated in online deliberations used different grammatical and narrative elements. Her team subsequently developed a coding scheme to analyze predictive, imperative, and subjunctive verb forms in these documents that they hand-coded using NVivo (see Chapter 7).

The mixed methods used by Franzosi, Cerulo, Roberts, Mische, and other sociologists are all, not surprisingly, basically sociological rather than only textual or contextual, as they involve research designs that allow for *deductive inferences* relating *strategically selected* texts to the societies in which they are produced and received (see Chapter 2).

Automated Methods of Narrative Analysis

Both qualitative and mixed methods narrative research are ultimately reliant on human interpretation and coding of texts. Such coding is sensitive to coder fatigue, intercoder reliability, and coder bias, and perhaps most importantly, it is time-intensive. The time required for training and coding has thus far limited researchers' ability to scale up narrative analysis for use with big data. But today this situation is changing, as at least one interdisciplinary research team is developing computer-assisted methods for automatically detecting narrative patterns in large text collections. Sudhahar and colleagues (2011) have developed a working system for large-scale quantitative narrative analysis of news corpora. Their system identifies the key actors in a body of news and the actions they perform by analyzing their positions in the overall network of actors and actions, analyzing the time series associated with some of the actors' properties, generating scatter plots describing the subject or object bias of each actor, and investigating the types of actions associated with each actor. Applying their automated system to 100,000 *New York Times* articles about crime published between 1987 and 2007, they found that men were most commonly responsible for crimes against the person, while women and children were most often crime victims.

Future Directions

Describing his experiences attending interdisciplinary conferences on narrative analysis, Franzosi (2012) wrote of the feeling of "having been involved in a dialogue if not among deaf, at least among skeptics or, better yet, among scholars who live in different worlds and simply do not understand each other" (p. 80). While narratologists and researchers who work with software and programming languages for text mining and analysis do sometimes appear to inhabit different worlds, recent research and the popularity of software packages for qualitative research (see next section) suggest that the fields of narratology and text analytics are gradually coming together and finding out what they can learn from one another.

Software for Narrative Analysis

Narrative analysis can be performed without the help of specialized software, but software can help to expand the scope, methodological sophistication, and rigor of narrative research. The most popular software packages used for narrative analysis are qualitative data analysis software (QDAS), which is reviewed in Chapter 7. Although QDAS programs with built-in statistical tools or statistical add-ons can be used for mixed methods narrative analysis, in the end these programs were designed for research that is basically qualitative. Mixed method research can generally benefit from more specialized software. Non-QDAS software tools that have been used in narrative analysis research include WordStat, which works with QDA Miner and offers key word in context (KWIC), key word retrieval, dictionary building, machine learning, and visualization capabilities (http://provalisresearch.com/products/content-analysis-software). WordSmith (http://www.lexically.net/wordsmith) is another useful and affordable package that offers KWIC, dictionary building, and word co-occurrences. And Franzosi, Doyle, McClelland, Putnam Rankin, and Vicari (2013) have developed PC-ACE (Program for Computer-Assisted Coding of Events; http://sociology.emory.edu/faculty/rfranzosi/pc-ace) specifically for narrative analysis of texts. The software is basically a free and open source relational database management tool.

9

Metaphor Analysis

●

Learning Objectives

The goals of Chapter 9 are to help readers do the following:

1. Understand the principles of cognitive metaphor theory.
2. Learn qualitative techniques for analyzing metaphorical language.
3. Learn about partially and fully automated methods for identifying and analyzing metaphors in large text collections.

I n this chapter, we review text analysis techniques that focus on metaphor. Much like narrative analysis, metaphor analysis techniques are used to gain insights into the divergent ways individuals and social groups come to interpret the social world. Whether taking the form of metaphor, analogy, simile, or synecdoche, metaphorical language involves figures of speech that make implicit comparisons in which a word or phrase ordinarily used in one domain is applied in another. While metaphor has long been a topic of literary scholarship, it was only in 1980 with the publication of George Lakoff and Mark Johnson's *Metaphors We Live By* that metaphor came to be an object of social science research. Lakoff and Johnson's (1980) approach to metaphor has come to be known as cognitive metaphor theory and has provided the conceptual foundation for the field of cognitive linguistics (Gibbs, 1994; Kovecses, 2002; Lakoff & Johnson, 1999; Sweetser, 1990).

We begin this chapter with a brief overview of cognitive metaphor theory, an approach to metaphor analysis developed by Lakoff, Johnson, and many of their fellow cognitive linguists that is based on the idea that language is structured by metaphor at a neural level and that metaphors used in natural language reveal cognitive schemas and associated patterns of neural connections shared by members of social groups. We review exemplary social science studies that use qualitative and mixed methods of metaphor analysis, focusing of course on these studies' research designs and methodologies. We also review promising recent efforts to automate the identification of metaphorical language in large text corpora. The chapter ends with a survey of software that has proven useful for metaphor analysis in social research.

Theoretical Foundations

The basic claim of cognitive metaphor theory is that metaphor is a central and indispensable structure of thought and language. All natural language is characterized by the presence of conventional metaphorical expressions organized around prototypical metaphors, which Lakoff and Johnson (1980) refer to as *conceptual metaphors*. These are linguistic expressions of the conventional pattern of thought of a group or society (Kovecses, 2002). For instance, Lakoff and Johnson argue that in many cultures people conceptualize *argument* in terms of a *battle*. This prototypical conceptual metaphor influences the way people talk about the act of arguing—for instance, when they use phrases such as "attack a position," "indefensible," "strategy," "new line of attack," "win," and "gain ground" (Lakoff & Johnson, 1980, p. 7).

According to cognitive metaphor theory, metaphors originate in a process of "phenomenological embodiment" (Lakoff & Johnson, 1999, p. 46). They are formed when perceptual and sensory experiences from an embodied *source domain*, such as pushing, pulling, supporting, balance, straight–curved, near–far, front–back, and high–low, are used to represent abstract entities in a *target domain* (Boroditsky, 2000; Lakoff, 1987; Richardson, Spivey, Barsalou, & McRae, 2003).

Cognitive metaphor theory is capable of explaining universal aspects of language and culture as well as cultural variation (Kovecses, 2002). While languages' phenomenological foundations are universal, societies and social groups differ in terms of the associations they make between conceptual metaphors and abstract target domains. In other words, different societies and groups use different sets of metaphors to construct and interpret social reality in different ways. An implication of cognitive metaphor theory for social research is that studying the distribution of metaphor in natural language can reveal how common sense is constructed and negotiated within groups.

Cognitive linguists themselves have studied metaphors used in natural language. For instance, both Lakoff (1996) and Chilton (1996) studied metaphors related to security used in political discourse. Charteris-Black (2009, 2012, 2013) has developed a rhetorically based approach to metaphor known as critical metaphor analysis that draws on methodologies and perspectives developed in cognitive linguistics, corpus linguistics, and critical linguistics. He has used the approach to examine metaphors from the domains of political rhetoric, press reporting, religion, and the communications of a wide range of political leaders. He has also worked jointly with sociologists on the relationship between gender, language, and illness narratives. And Goatly (2007) investigated how conceptual metaphor shapes thought and behavior in fields including architecture, engineering, education, genetics, ecology, economics, politics, industrial time-management, medicine, immigration, race, and sex. He argues that the ideologies of early capitalism used metaphor themes historically traceable through Hobbes, Hume, Smith, Malthus, and Darwin and that these metaphorical concepts support neo-Darwinian and neoconservative ideologies up to the present day. Hart (2010) has advocated for a cognitive linguistic approach to critical discourse analysis (see Chapter 2). Hart's approach involves a semantic analysis of particular lexical, grammatical, and pragmatic features found in political and media discourse. More narrowly, it investigates the conceptual structures that are associated with different language usages and the ideological functions that such structures may serve. He has applied this framework primarily in the context of anti-immigration discourse (Hart, 2010).

While the critical natural language studies of metaphor by Chilton, Charteris-Black, Goatly, Hart, and Lakoff are innovative and important contributions, their impact has been mainly felt in linguistics rather than in the social sciences. But social researchers working in the fields of anthropology, education, management, political science, psychology, sociology, and other fields have used cognitive metaphor theory in text mining and analysis projects of their own. We review some of this work in the next sections, starting with qualitative studies and then covering mixed methods research.

Qualitative Metaphor Analysis

In the social sciences, metaphor analysis is a semantic text analysis technique concerned with latent meaning rather than a thematic technique concerned with the manifest meaning of text (Roberts, 1997). Influenced by cognitive metaphor theory, researchers from anthropology, education, management, psychology, and sociology have developed a number of methods of qualitative metaphor analysis.

Anthropology

There is much anthropological literature on metaphor, although most anthropological studies use ethnographic rather than text mining or text analysis methods. James Fernandez's 1991 edited collection *Beyond Metaphor* provides a good overview of early ethnographic work in this area, and cognitive anthropologists Dorothy Holland and Naomi Quinn's 1987 classic *Cultural Models in Language and Thought* was a breakthrough in terms of connecting anthropology to cognitive linguistics and cognitive metaphor theory (see also Strauss & Quinn, 1997). Some of the work on metaphor done by anthropologists does employ text analysis techniques, such as Strauss's (1997) study of what industrial workers and their neighbors think about the free enterprise system, Quinn's (1996) studies of metaphors used by Americans in talking about their marriages, and Kempton's (1987) study of Americans' lay theories of home heat control.

Educational Research

Cameron (2003) and other educational researchers have used cognitive metaphor theory to analyze figurative language used by students and teachers in classroom settings. More recently Rees, Knight, and Wilkinson (2007) analyzed metaphors in strategically collected transcripts of patients', medical students', and doctors' discussions of doctor–patient interactions. The data for their qualitative and inductive study were from multiple document collections, including focus group discussions with patients, medical students and medical educators. Their analysis revealed six prototypical metaphors associated with the target domain of student and doctor–patient relationships: the relationship as war, hierarchy, doctor-centeredness, market, machine, and theater. All of the metaphors except the theater metaphor emphasized the oppositional quality of student and doctor–patient relationships.

Political Science

As part of the rhetorical turn in political science (see Beer & Hariman, 1996), researchers have turned to metaphorical language in policy documents, speeches, and other political texts to explore the ways metaphors mediate relations between countries and other political actors. For example, the edited collection *Metaphorical World Politics* (Beer & De Landtsheer, 2004) includes chapters on the metaphors that have guided and shaped American foreign policy in the public arena since the start of the Cold War. The studies in this collection cover metaphors for democracy, war and peace, and globalization. The chapters' authors analyze sports metaphors in Desert Storm discourse, disease metaphors used during the Cold War for the threat of communism, and path metaphors used in deliberations over U.S. foreign policy toward Cambodia, among other conceptual metaphors (see also Carver & Pikalo, 2008). Methodologically, most political science studies of metaphor are basically qualitative, although there have been some mixed methods studies as well (e.g., De Landtsheer & De Vrij, 2004).

Psychology

Clinical psychologists have analyzed metaphors used by subjects in psychoanalytic therapy (Buchholz & von Kleist, 1995; Roderburg, 1998), and cognitive and experimental psychologists have studied metaphors as examples of mental models (Johnson-Laird, 1983, 1989). But within psychology, only Schmitt (2000, 2005) has developed a qualitative method of text analysis centered on metaphor. Schmitt's (2000) "rule-based and step-by-step approach" (p. 2) is idiographic and qualitative and is based on inductive inferential logic. It operates at a sociological level of analysis that involves making inferences about the community that generates the text being analyzed and involves a multiple-document-collection data selection strategy. The goal of Schmitt's (2000) method of systematic metaphor analysis is to "discover sub-cultural thinking patterns" (p. 365), and his method accomplishes this in several steps. The first step is for the researcher to choose a topic of analysis. Schmitt (2000) gave the example of abstinence from his own empirical work on metaphors for abstinence and alcoholism. The next step is to assemble a "broad-based collection of background metaphors" (Schmitt, 2005, p. 370) for the topic. These metaphors can be collected from sources such as encyclopedias, journals, and specialist and generalist books. In Schmitt's own work, background metaphors include metaphors for the effects of drinking alcohol such as being more "open" versus "fencing off" from others. The third step is to analyze the metaphors used in the natural language of the subgroup. This involves creating the second document collection, identifying metaphors in that collection, and then reconstructing metaphorical concepts from those metaphors. The fourth and final step is to compare the metaphorical concepts from the two document collections in order to learn about the culture and psychology of the subgroup in comparison to the culture and psychology of the general population.

Sociology

Similar to the work of the linguist Christopher Hart, in *Brown Tide Rising* (2002) the sociologist Otto Santa Ana (2002) combined critical discourse analysis (Chapter 2) and metaphor analysis. Santa Ana's data are newspapers that he used to study mass media representations of Latinos in the United States.

More recently, the sociologists Schuster, Beune, and Stronks (2011) have studied metaphorical constructions of hypertension among ethnic groups in the Netherlands. Rather than using secondary data, as is the case for most of the studies reviewed previously, Schuster and colleagues (2011) collected their own data by transcribing interviews they performed with members of three ethnic groups in the Netherlands. Their approach is basically inductive and involves constructing multiple corpora translated from different languages.

Mixed Methods of Metaphor Analysis

Social researchers have developed a number of mixed methods strategies for metaphor analysis. Generally, these involve human coding of metaphors in combination with statistical tests for both interrater reliability and differences in rates of metaphor use across multiple document collections. The document collections are typically produced by social groups with different social or cultural backgrounds. Where qualitative metaphor analysis (e.g., Santa Ana, 2002; Schmitt, 2005) is mostly inductive, mixed methods research is mostly deductive, although it often involves abductive inference as well (see Chapter 2).

Management Research

Management researchers Gibson and Zellmer-Bruhn (2001) used a mixed method of metaphor analysis to study concepts of teamwork across national organizational cultures. Their theory-driven project used a deductive inferential logic, featured a research design with multiple corpora, and operated at a sociological level of analysis in that the researchers analyzed texts for the purpose of learning about the organizations and societies that produced them. This study's goal was to test a well-known theory of the influence of national culture on employees' attitudes (Hofstede, 1980). Gibson and Zellmer-Bruhn (2001) tested this theory with a research design that included strategic selection first of four nations (France, the Philippines, Puerto Rico, and the United States) and then of four organizations based on Hofstede's theory (p. 281). The researchers conducted interviews that they transcribed to form their corpora, which they analyzed using QSR NUD*IST (Qualitative Solutions and Research, 1997) and TACT (Bradley, 1989; Popping, 1997). These software packages were used to organize the qualitative coding of five frequently used teamwork metaphors, which were then used to create dependent variables for hypothesis testing using multinomial logit and logistic regression.

Psychology

The social psychologist Karin Moser (2000) has developed a metaphor-based method of text analysis that she has applied in her research on the psychology of work and organizations. Moser's mixed methods approach involves categorizing metaphors for the self during transitions from school to work. The self-concept is highly complex and abstract and is thus often represented with metaphors. The subjects Moser studied were Swiss German students who participated in a questionnaire study about their anticipated transition from university to work. A subsample of 12 students was included in the study and interviewed about their experiences with success and relationship quality and their expectations and wishes for the future. The transcribed interviews were analyzed thematically and for self-metaphors and other aspects of the students' self-concepts. Her quantitative analysis of this data revealed statistically significant relationships between themes and metaphors and between metaphors and self-concepts. There was a general preference for scientific and technological metaphors, followed by container, path, visual, balance, war, and economic metaphors. Metaphor use is also significantly influenced by social variables such as the general orientation toward the future; the field of study; and, to a smaller extent, gender.

Sociology

The sociologist Ignatow has developed mixed methods of metaphor analysis in studies of high-tech jargon (2003), transcripts of shipyard workers' meetings (2004), and discussions by members of online self-help groups (2009). His mixed method approach is nomothetic and based on deductive inference, operates at a sociological level of analysis, and involves both strategic selection of and statistical sampling from multiple document collections (with the exception of the 2004 study). He uses metaphor analysis in combination with other text analysis methods such as narrative analysis (2004; see Chapter 8) and semantic network analysis (2009) to test theories related to culture and to the work of the sociologist Pierre Bourdieu. Software used includes TextAnalyst and the statistical packages Stata and SPSS.

Automated Metaphor Identification Methods

Both qualitative and mixed methods metaphor research are ultimately reliant on human interpretation and coding of metaphors in texts. Such coding is subject to coder fatigue, coder bias, and problems of coder interrater reliability. It is also time-intensive, and the time required for training and coding has thus far limited researchers' ability to scale up metaphor analysis for use with big data. But today, the situation is changing rapidly, as several research teams in computer science and related fields are developing computer-assisted methods for automatically detecting metaphors in texts.

Early attempts by Fass (1991) and more recent work by Mason (2004) relied on predefined semantic and domain knowledge to attempt to identify metaphor in texts. Birke and Sarkar (2007) approached the problem by considering literal and nonliteral usages to be different senses of a single word. Hardie, Koller, Rayson, and Semino (2007) repurposed semantic annotation tools in order to extract possibly metaphoric phrases from texts. Turney, Neuman, Assaf, and Cohen (2011) identified metaphorical phrases by assuming that these phrases consist of both a more concrete and a more abstract term. They derived an algorithm to define the abstractness of a term and then used this algorithm to contrast the abstractness of adjective–noun phrases. Phrases were labeled as metaphorical when the difference between the abstractness of the noun and the abstractness of the adjective passed a predetermined threshold.

Recently, Gandy, Neuman, and their colleagues (Gandy et al., 2013; Neuman et al. 2013) have developed a number of interrelated algorithms that have been able to identify metaphorical language in texts with a high level of accuracy. Their work is based on Turney and colleagues' (2011) key insight that a metaphor usually involves a mapping from a concrete domain to a more abstract domain. The algorithms are thus based on a target noun's abstractness and its accompanying adjective's number of dictionary definitions (if there is only one, the adjective cannot be part of a metaphor). If none of the most common concrete nouns that are commonly associated with the adjective are present, the target noun is coded as metaphorical.

The results so far of these efforts by computational linguists to automate metaphor extraction suggest to us that there is great potential for automated methods of metaphor analysis to be used in social science text mining and analysis applications in the near future.

Software for Metaphor Analysis

Many of the software tools and packages reviewed in Part II can be used for metaphor analysis as well as for narrative analysis, including QDAS (qualitative data analysis software) packages such as ATLAS.ti (http://atlasti.com; see Kalo & Racz, 2014), MAXQDA (http://www.maxqda.com), and NVivo (http://www.qsrinternational.com/product).

Text Mining Methods From Computer Science

PART IV

10

Word and Text Relatedness

Learning Objectives

The goals of Chapter 10 are to help readers do the following:

1. Understand the goals and applications of the task of word and text relatedness.
2. Learn about corpus-based and knowledge-based measures of word relatedness.
3. Learn how to build upon word relatedness to create measures of text relatedness.

Semantic relatedness involves identification and quantification of the strength of semantic connections that exist between textual units, be they word pairs, sentence pairs, or document pairs. When we make judgments about semantic connections in everyday life, we typically rely on our accumulated knowledge and experiences and utilize our capacities for conceptual thinking, abstraction, and generalization. Modeling semantic relatedness is one of the main tasks of the field of natural language processing and lies at the core of a large number of applications such as information retrieval (Ponte & Croft, 1998), query reformulation (Broder et al., 2008; Metzler, Dumais, & Meek, 2007; Sahami & Heilman, 2006; Yih & Meek, 2007), image retrieval (Goodrum, 2000; Leong & Mihalcea, 2009), plagiarism detection (Brin, Davis, & Garca-Molina, 1995; Broder, Glassman, Manasse, & Zweig, 1997; Heintze, 1996; Hoad & Zobel, 2003; Manber, 1994; Shivakumar & Garcia-Molina, 1995), sponsored search (Broder et al., 2008), short-answer grading (Mitchell, Russell, Broomhead, & Aldridge, 2002; Mohler & Mihalcea, 2009; Pulman & Sukkarieh, 2005), and textual entailment (Dagan, Glickman, & Magnini, 2005).

In this chapter, we first provide an overview of several corpus- and knowledge-based measures of word-based relatedness. We then show how these word-based measures can be combined into a text-based measure and conclude with a discussion of applications of word and text relatedness to social research.

Theoretical Foundations

A relatively large number of word-to-word relatedness metrics have been proposed in the natural language processing literature. These range from distance-based measures computed on semantic networks or taxonomies, to metrics based on models of distributional similarity learned from large text collections. For instance, one may wish to determine how semantically related are *car* and *automobile*, or *noon* and *string*. Here we focus our attention on three corpus-based and six knowledge-based metrics, which we selected mainly for their wide use and good performance in natural language–processing applications.

Although measures of semantic relatedness have been traditionally defined between words or concepts, it is often important to determine the relatedness of text segments consisting of two or more words. For example, one may want to find the relatedness of two pieces of text such as "I love animals" versus "I own a pet." The emphasis on word-to-word relatedness metrics is probably due to the availability of resources that specifically encode relations between words or concepts (e.g., WordNet) and the various test-beds that allow for their evaluation (e.g., TOEFL or SAT analogy/synonymy tests). Nonetheless, text-to-text measures of relatedness have also been proposed, often starting with a word-based semantic relatedness metric.

A difference is often made between semantic *relatedness* and semantic *similarity*. Similarity is a more specific concept than relatedness: Similarity is concerned with entities related by virtue of their likeness and that stay within a part of speech boundary—for example, *bank–trust company*, however dissimilar entities may also be related, e.g., *hot–cold, hiking–mountain, and food–sea*. A full treatment of the topic can be found in Budanitsky and Hirst (2001). In this chapter, we mostly address the more general task of relatedness, but also include references to work concerned with word and text similarity.

Corpus-Based and Knowledge-Based Measures of Relatedness

Corpus-Based Measures of Word Relatedness

Corpus-based measures of word semantic similarity try to identify the degree of similarity between words using information exclusively derived from large corpora. There are three corpus-based measures that have been used more frequently: (1) pointwise mutual information (PMI; Turney, 2001), (2) latent semantic analysis (LSA; Landauer, Foltz, & Laham, 1998), and (3) explicit semantic analysis (ESA; Gabrilovich & Markovitch, 2007).

Pointwise Mutual Information The PMI using data collected by information retrieval (PMI-IR) was suggested by Turney (2001) as an unsupervised measure for the evaluation of the semantic similarity of words. It is based on word co-occurrence using counts collected over very large corpora (e.g., the web). Given two words w_1 and w_2, their PMI-IR is measured as the following:

$$PMI - IR(w_1, w_2) = \log \frac{p(w_1 \& w_2)}{p(w_1) * p(w_2)}$$

This indicates the degree of statistical dependence between w_1 and w_2 and can be used as a measure of the semantic similarity of w_1 and w_2.

With $p(w_i)$ approximated as hits(w_i)/WebSize, the following PMI-IR measure is obtained:

$$PMI - IR(w_1, w_2) = \log_2 \frac{hits(w_1 AND w_2) * WebSize}{hits(w_1) * hits(w_2)}$$

In general, since we care about a ranking over the relatedness of several word pairs, the WebSize value is irrelevant in the ranking. When an absolute value of the relatedness is necessary, we can use a very large value to approximate WebSize.

Latent Semantic Analysis Another corpus-based measure of semantic similarity is LSA, proposed by Landauer and colleagues (1998). In LSA, term co-occurrences in a corpus are captured by means of a dimensionality reduction operated by a singular value decomposition (SVD) on the term-by-document matrix T representing the corpus.

SVD is a well-known operation in linear algebra, which can be applied to any rectangular matrix in order to find correlations among its rows and columns. In our case, SVD decomposes the term-by-document matrix T into three matrices $T = U\Sigma_k V^T$ where Σ_k is the diagonal k × k matrix containing the k singular values of T, $\sigma_1 \geq \sigma_2 \geq \ldots \geq \sigma_k$, and U and V are column-orthogonal matrices. When the three matrices are multiplied together, the original term-by-document matrix is recomposed. Typically we can choose $k' \ll k$ obtaining the approximation $T \simeq U\Sigma_{k'}' V^T$.

LSA can be viewed as a way to overcome some of the drawbacks of the standard vector space model (see Chapter 13: Information Retrieval), namely sparseness and high dimensionality. In fact, the LSA similarity is computed in a lower dimensional space, in which second-order relations among terms and texts are exploited.

The similarity in the resulting vector space is then measured with the standard cosine similarity. Note also that LSA yields a vector space model that allows for a *homogeneous* representation (and hence comparison) of words, word sets, and texts.

Explicit Semantic Analysis Another corpus-based measure of relatedness that is frequently used is ESA (Gabrilovich & Markovitch, 2007), which uses encyclopedic knowledge found in Wikipedia in an information retrieval framework to generate a semantic interpretation of words. ESA relies on the distribution of words inside the encyclopedic descriptions. Since encyclopedic knowledge is typically organized into concepts (or topics), each concept is further described using definitions and examples. ESA takes advantage of this organization by building semantic representations for a given word using a word-concept association, where the concept represents a Wikipedia article. In this vector representation, the semantic interpretation of a word is modeled as a semantic vector consisting of all the concepts (Wikipedia articles) in which the word appears weighted by its occurrence frequency. Furthermore, the semantic interpretation of a text fragment can be modeled as an aggregation of the semantic vectors of its individual words. Such representation reduces any inherent ambiguity in the text fragment introduced by polysemous terms and promotes context relevant concepts in the feature space. In this vector representation, each encyclopedic concept is assigned a weight, calculated as the tf.idf (term frequency–inverse document frequency) of the given word inside the concept's article. Formally, let c be the set of all the Wikipedia concepts, and let a be any content word. We define the ESA concept vector of term a:

$$\{\langle w_1, c_1 \rangle, \langle w_2, c_2 \rangle \ldots \langle w_n, c_n \rangle\}$$

Therefore, w_i is the weight of the concept c_i with respect to a. ESA assumes the weight w_i to be the term frequency tf_i of the word a in the article corresponding to concept c_i.

The ESA semantic relatedness between the words in a given word pair is then measured as the cosine similarity between their corresponding vectors.

Word Embeddings One of the most recent methods to measure word relatedness is based on word embeddings, which are deep learning vectors learned using a skip-gram recurrent neural net architecture running over a large raw corpus (Mikolov, Yih, & Zweig, 2013). A primary advantage of word embeddings is that, by breaking away from the typical n-gram model that sees individual units with no relationship to one other, they are to generalize and produce word vectors that are similar for related words, thus encoding linguistic regularities and patterns. For example, assuming that the function vector() returns the word embedding for an input word, it has been shown that vector("Madrid")-vector("Spain")+vector("France") is closer to vector("Paris") than any other word vector. Google has made available a pretrained word embedding model called word2vec, which is built over a 100 billion-word corpus, and contains 3 million 300-dimension vectors for words and phrases.

Knowledge-Based Measures of Word Relatedness

There are a number of measures that were developed to quantify the degree to which two words are semantically related using information drawn from semantic networks—see, for example, Budanitsky and Hirst (2001) for an overview. We next present several measures found to work well on the WordNet hierarchy: Jiang and Conrath (1997); Leacock, Chodorow, and Miller (1998); Lesk (1986); Lin (1998); Resnik (1995); and Wu and Palmer (1994). Note that all of these metrics are defined between senses, rather than words, but they can be easily turned into a word-to-word similarity metric by selecting for any given pair of words those two meanings that lead to the highest sense-to-sense similarity.

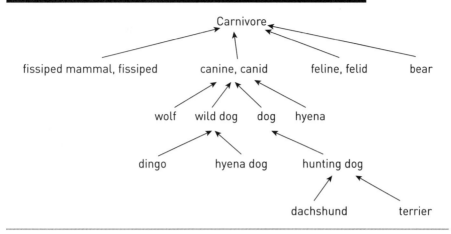

FIGURE 10.1 ● Sample Snapshot From a Semantic Hierarchy

The Leacock and Chodorow (1998) similarity is determined as the following:

$$\mathrm{Rel}_{lch} = -\log \frac{length}{2 * D}$$

Length is the length of the shortest path between two senses using node counting, and D is the maximum depth of the taxonomy. For instance, considering the semantic hierarchy snapshot from Figure 10.1, the shortest path between dingo and hyena dog is 3, and the maximum depth of the hierarchy is 4.

The Lesk similarity of two senses is defined as a function of the overlap between the corresponding definitions, as provided by a dictionary. It is based on an algorithm proposed by Lesk (1986) as a solution for word sense disambiguation. The application of the Lesk similarity measure is not limited to semantic networks, and it can be used in conjunction with any dictionary that provides word definitions.

The Wu and Palmer (1994) similarity metric measures the depth of two given senses in the WordNet taxonomy and the depth of the least common subsumer (LCS)[1] and combines these figures into a similarity score:

$$\mathrm{Rel}_{wup} = \frac{2 * depth(LCS)}{depth(sense\_a) + depth(sense\_b)}$$

---

1. The LCS of two input concepts is the most specific concept in the hierarchy that subsumes the two input concepts. For instance, in Figure 10.1, *canine, canid* is the LCS of *dingo* and *hyena dog*.

The measure introduced by Resnik (1995) returns the information content (IC) of the LCS of two senses:

$$Rel_{res} = IC(LCS)$$

IC is defined as the following:

$$IC(c) = -\log P(c)$$

P(c) is the probability of encountering an instance of sense c in a large corpus.

Two other metrics that build upon Resnik's measure of similarity are Lin (1998), which adds a normalization factor consisting of the IC of the two input senses:

$$Rel_{lin} = \frac{2 * IC(LCS)}{IC(sense_a) + IC(sense_b)}$$

Jiang and Conrath (1997) introduced an alternative interpretation of semantic relatedness by discounting the IC of the LCS of $sense_a$ and $sense_b$ from the IC of the individual senses:

$$Rel_{lin} = \frac{1}{IC(sense_a) + IC(sense_b) - 2 * IC(LCS)}$$

Note that all the word relatedness measures are normalized so that they fall within a 0 to 1 range. The normalization is done by dividing the relatedness score provided by a given measure with the maximum possible score for that measure.

Measures of Text Relatedness

One of the earliest applications of text relatedness is perhaps the vector space model in information retrieval (see Chapter 13: Information Retrieval, where the document most relevant to an input query is determined by ranking documents in a collection in reversed order of their relatedness to the given query; Salton & Lesk, 1971). Text relatedness has also been used for relevance feedback and text classification Rocchio (1971), word sense disambiguation (Lesk, 1986; Schutze, 1998), and more recently for extractive summarization (Salton, Singhal, Mitra, & Buckley, 1997) and methods for automatic evaluation of machine translation (Papineni, Roukos, Ward, & Zhu, 2002) or text summarization (Lin & Hovy, 2003).

With few exceptions, the typical approach to finding the relatedness between two text segments is to use a simple lexical-matching method and produce a related-ness score based on the number of lexical units that occur in both input segments. Improvements to this simple method have considered stemming, stop word removal, part of speech tagging, longest subsequence matching, as well as various weighting and normalization factors (Salton & Buckley, 1988). While successful to a certain degree, these lexical relatedness methods cannot always identify the *semantic* relatedness of texts. For instance, there is an obvious relatedness between the text segments "We own a pet" and "I love animals," but most of the lexical-matching text relatedness metrics will fail in identifying any kind of connection between these texts.

More recently, a newly proposed text-to-text relatedness method (Hassan & Mihalcea, 2011; Islam & Inkpen, 2009; Mihalcea, Corley, & Strapparava, 2006) utilizes a bipartite–graph matching strategy to aggregate word-to-word relatedness between text constituents into one text relatedness score.

In addition to the relatedness of words, these methods generally take into account the specificity of words so that a higher weight is given to a semantic matching identified between two specific words (e.g., *collie* and *sheepdog*) and less importance is given to the relatedness measured between generic concepts (e.g., *get* and *become*). While the specificity of words is already measured to some extent by their depth in the semantic hierarchy, they are reinforced with a corpus-based measure of word specificity, based on distributional information learned from large corpora.

The specificity of a word is determined using the inverse document frequency (*idf*) introduced by Sparck-Jones (1972), defined as the total number of documents in the corpus divided by the total number of documents including that word. The idf measure was selected based on previous work that theoretically proved the effectiveness of this weighting approach (Papineni, 2001).

In Hassan and Mihalcea (2011), given SSA_{cos} or SSA_{soc} as metric for word-to-word relatedness, the relatedness of two text segments T_a and T_b can be calculated as follows: Each word w in the segment T_a is paired with the word in the segment T_b that has the highest semantic relatedness in a mutually exclusive manner. The relatedness scores of the aligned pairs are then aggregated to produce text relatedness score.

Formally, let T_a and T_b be two text fragments of size *a* and *b* respectively. After removing all stop words, let (ω) be the number of shared terms between T_a and T_b. The semantic relatedness of all possible pairings between nonshared terms in T_a and T_b is calculated using word-to-word relatedness method. The best possible pairs are selected in set ϕ, which holds the strongest semantic pairings between the fragments' terms, such that each term can belong to one and only one pair. The semantic relatedness between the two text fragments can be expressed as the following:

$$\mathrm{Re}l(T_a, T_b) = \frac{\left(\varpi + \sum_{i=1}^{|\varphi|} \varphi_i\right) * (2ab)}{a+b}$$

Therefore, ω is the number of shared terms between the text fragments and φ_i is the relatedness score for the ith pairing.

Mihalcea and colleagues (2006) dropped the mutual exclusivity condition, hence different pairs emerge based on the reference text fragment. Given a input metric for word-to-word similarity and a measure of word specificity, each word w in the segment T_1 is aligned with word in the segment T_2 that has the highest semantic relatedness (maxRel(w,T_2)). Next, the same process is applied to determine the most similar word in T_1 starting with words in T_2. The word similarities are then weighted with the corresponding word specificity, summed up, and normalized with the length of each text segment.

The relatedness between the input text segments T_1 and T_2 is therefore determined using the following scoring function:

$$sim(T_1, T_2) = \frac{1}{2} \left(\frac{\sum\limits_{w \in \{T_1\}} \max Rel(w, T_2) * idf(w)}{\sum\limits_{w \in \{T_1\}} idf(w)} + \frac{\sum\limits_{w \in \{T_2\}} \max Rel(w, T_1) * idf(w)}{\sum\limits_{w \in \{T_2\}} idf(w)} \right)$$

Recent years have seen a surge of interest in textual similarity, with several community-wide evaluations being organized for text-to-text similarity (Agirre, Cer, Diab, Gonzalez-Agirre, & Guo, 2013). The SemEval/*SEM proceedings include a number of papers describing various text-to-text similarity systems. There is also a growing body of work concerned with word and text similarity for other languages; see, for instance, the cross-lingual similarity method proposed in Hassan & Mihalcea (2009) or the systems participating in the Spanish text similarity task organized at SemEval 2014 (Banea, Mihalcea, Cardie, & Wiebe, 2014).

Software and Data Sets for Word and Text Relatedness

WordNet::Similarity (http://wn-similarity.sourceforge.net) is a Perl package that implements several word relatedness measures on WordNet. NLTK (http://www.nltk .org) also includes a number of relatedness measures on WordNet, implemented in Python. Gensim (https://pypi.python.org/pypi/gensim) is a Python implementation of LSA. word2vec (https://code.google.com/p/word2vec) is a pretrained word-embedding model made available by Google, containing 3 million 300-dimension vectors for words and phrases.

There are three data sets that are widely used for word-to-word relatedness: Rubenstein and Goodenough (Rubenstein & Goodenough, 1965) consists of 65 word pairs ranging from synonymy pairs (e.g., car–automobile) to completely unrelated terms (e.g., noon–string). The 65 noun pairs were annotated by 51 human subjects. Miller–Charles (Miller & Charles, 1998) is a subset of the Rubenstein and Goodenough data set, consisting of 30 word pairs. The relatedness of each word pair was rated by 38 human subjects, using the same scale as just given. WordSimilarity-353 (Finkelstein et al., 2001), also known as Finkelstein-353, consists of 353 word pairs annotated by 13 human experts.

Evaluations of text-to-text similarity measures are mainly done under the SemEval exercises (http://alt.qcri.org/semeval2016; http://alt.qcri.org/semeval2015), which provide several data sets consisting of pairs of texts manually annotated for similarity. Evaluations have been run for sentence-level English and Spanish similarity and for cross-level (e.g., word-to-phrase, sentence-to-paragraph) English similarity. Earlier data sets for the evaluation of text-to-text similarity measures are Lee50 (Lee, Pincombe, & Welsh, 2005), Li30 (Li, McLean, Bandar, O'Shea, & Crockett, 2006), AG400 (Mohler & Mihalcea, 2009), and Microsoft paraphrase corpus (Dolan, Quirk, & Brockett, 2004).

11

Text Classification

●

Learning Objectives

The goals of Chapter 11 are to help readers do the following:

1. Understand the task of text classification and learn about its applications.

2. Learn about the representations used to enable supervised algorithms for text classification.

3. Learn about text classification algorithms.

4. Learn about available software packages for automatic text classification.

Text classification (sometimes also referred to as text categorization) is the task of assigning texts with one or more predefined categories. An example of text classification at work is e-mail spam detection, where the text classifier automatically assigns each incoming e-mail with one of the predefined categories (i.e., spam or no spam).

Formally, given a representation R of a text T—and given a fixed set of categories $C = \{C_1, C_2, \ldots, C_n\}$—the task of text classification is to determine a mapping from R to a category in C. This is typically done by learning how to make such mappings from a set of texts that have been already mapped to categories in C. This is referred to as training data and is used to learn associations between their representations and the C categories. In the e-mail spam example, assuming that the representation R used for the texts consists of the words in those texts, a possible association that a classifier would learn could be, for instance, that *mortgage* and *interest* are more often associated with spam e-mail than legitimate e-mail, whereas *dinner* and *baby* would occur more frequently in non-spam e-mails.

Categories can often be hierarchical, as, for instance, in the case of the categories in Figure 11.1, which represent a possible classification of a number of areas in artificial intelligence.

It is important to differentiate between text classification and text clustering. The latter refers to the task of grouping texts into categories; however, in text clustering the categories are not known a priori. Given a set of texts, a clustering system will identify that certain texts are more similar to one another than others and should

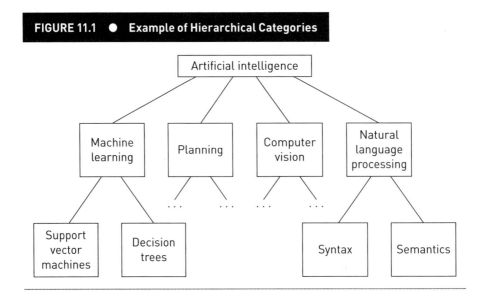

FIGURE 11.1 ● Example of Hierarchical Categories

be assigned to the same cluster, but it will not give a name to this cluster. Moreover, the number of clusters that a collection of texts will be split into is often not known. Thus, text classification is often thought of as a supervised task, whereas text clustering is often unsupervised (as with anything, there are exceptions, as there are text classification methods that are unsupervised and text clustering methods that are supervised).

A Brief History of Text Classification

In the early days, the classification of texts was done manually by "domain experts" who were familiar with the topics of the texts being classified. This was, for instance, the approach taken by Yahoo when creating their "browsing" capability: Each new webpage was manually assigned with one or more categories. As expected, this classification approach was highly accurate, in particular when the data set was relatively small and the team of experts categorizing documents was also small (so as to avoid inconsistency among annotators). But the approach quickly became intractable, as the number of documents that needed to be classified grew to a very large number (webpages in the case of Yahoo!).

The next step in the history of text classification was rule-based systems, which used queries consisting of combinations of words to determine the category of a text. For instance, if a text included the words *bank* and *money* and *interest*, there could be a rule that would say that this text was part of the financial domain.

LexisNexis, for instance, used such rule-based systems using complex query languages. The accuracy of these systems was generally very high, but they once again suffered from a scalability issue because building and maintaining these rules was an expensive process.

After this, machine learning came into the picture, and supervised or semi-supervised learning became the de facto approach for text classification. There are currently numerous algorithms that are available for automatic classification, ranging from nearest neighbor and Naive Bayes to decision trees and support vector machines (SVMs). These systems come at the cost of annotated data, which is required to train the supervised algorithms, but they have the benefit of scalability, as once trained they can be used to classify essentially any amount of unlabeled data.

Applications of Text Classification

Text classification is one of the most widely used applications of text mining or artificial intelligence. The following are just a handful of examples of text classification applied to real-life problems.

Topic Classification

Topic classification is used to categorize documents by their topics, be it computer science, music, or biology (McCallum and Nigam, 1998). This task is often used to organize web texts (see the Open Directory Project [http://www.dmoz.org], where millions of webpages are organized into a hierarchy of categories such as fitness, software, and real estate). Table 11.1 shows one example of a text from the topic of computer science (left) and another from the topic of music (right).

TABLE 11.1 ● Examples of Texts Classified by Topic

As a discipline, computer science spans a range of topics from theoretical studies of algorithms and the limits of computation to the practical issues of implementing computing systems in hardware and software. The Association for Computing Machinery (ACM) and the IEEE Computer Society (IEEE-CS) identify four areas: theory of computation, algorithms and data structures, programming methodology and languages, and computer elements and architecture.	The notes of the 12-tone scale can be written by their letter names A to G, possibly with a trailing sharp or flat symbol, such as A♯ or B♭. This is the most common way of specifying a note in English speech or written text. In Northern and Central Europe, the letter system used is slightly different for historical reasons. In these countries' languages, the note called simply B in English (i.e., B♮) is called H, and the note B♭ is named B.
Computer science	Music

TABLE 11.2 ● Legitimate E-Mail and Spam E-Mail	
Hi John,	Dear John Doe,
I hope you are doing well. Have you found a job after your graduation?	ICISA (International Conference on Information Science and Applications) has been scheduled from May 6th to 9th, 2014, in Seoul, South Korea. The final paper submission date is **February 28, 2014.** Please make sure to submit your paper before this date! With IEEE, ICISA will be holding its fifth annual conference. The ICISA 2014 paper submission system is now open and ready for you to upload your paper.
I was wondering if you could tell me where the web camera is that you used for the emotion detection experiments? Is it still in Dr. Yong's lab? I had borrowed it from Prof. Doe in the CSE department, and I should eventually return it to him at some point.	
Legitimate e-mail	Spam e-mail

E-Mail Spam Detection

This is perhaps the most ubiquitous application of text classification, being in use every day by practically all the users of an e-mail service. Spam detectors usually run "behind the scenes" in any e-mail server and run on top of the stream of incoming e-mails to determine whether an e-mail should be sent to the user's inbox or to the spam folder. This is an application where it is very important to keep the rate of false positives very low even if it comes at the cost of some false negatives. In other words, one would ideally want to avoid losing any legitimate e-mail to the spam folder, even if some spam e-mail makes it to the user's inbox. This constraint also dictates some of the parameter settings used for text classification for spam detection, with only high-confidence spam being filtered out. Table 11.2 shows an example of a legitimate e-mail and a spam e-mail.

Sentiment Analysis/Opinion Mining

An application that has received an increasing amount of attention during recent years is that of sentiment analysis (also referred to as opinion mining [Mihalcea, Banea, & Wiebe, 2007; Pang & Lee, 2008; Wiebe, Wilson, & Cardie, 2005]). The classification is performed between positive and negative sentiment and is used to detect consumer sentiment for given products (e.g., Is this a positive or a negative review of a smartphone?), to monitor a company's brand, to detect product/service issues for targeted customer service, and so on. Table 11.3 shows examples of a positive and a negative review of the movie *Big Hero 6*.

Gender Classification

Text classification is also used for tasks aimed at "author profiling"—that is, determining the age, gender, or political orientation of the author of a text (Koppel, Argamon, & Shimoni, 2002; Liu & Mihalcea, 2007). While text classification also has

TABLE 11.3 ● Positive and Negative Reviews of the Movie *Big Hero 6*	
I actually wasn't planning to watch this particular movie, until my friends told me it was a good movie and that I should watch it. I decided to try it and see how it goes. I instantly fell in love with Baymax. He's huggable and simply adorable. Along with that, he's a HEALTHCARE companion! It was certainly a HILARIOUS movie, and I enjoyed every last bit of it. All I have to say is that this movie is definitely one worth watching, especially if you like humorous animated films.	I hate this movie for having one of the most cookie-cutter plots imaginable and for trying to build tension where there is none. I am tired of kid's movies trying to be something they're not. You can only have so much drama, because only so many things can possibly happen in a kids movie. This isn't *Breaking Bad* or *Django*. Baymax isn't going to snap and kill anyone. It just won't happen ever. So why would the movie pretend it could happen. All this fake drama that leads to nothing makes for a very boring and hollow movie.
Positive review	Negative review

been applied to more traditional texts such as books or other works of fiction, the interest in author profiling has grown with the explosion of social media. It is an interesting task not only for what it achieves but also because it is one of the few examples in artificial intelligence where a computer performs better than a human. Consider the example of texts written by a man or a woman illustrated in Table 11.4. As it turns out, people generally have a hard time figuring out whether a text was written by man or by a woman, mainly because some of the most useful clues to gender detection consist of function words (such as *we* or *of*), which we do not naturally pay attention to. Computers instead do better at this task, as they are not used, as we are, to focusing their "attention" on content words only, and instead can quickly count the function words that are useful for this classification task.

TABLE 11.4 ● Texts Written by a Woman and a Man	
Spring at Wellington! Or was it summer?? Oh, who cares . . . summer felt like winter the last time around—especially when things, ahem, didn't quite worked out as planned. Grr! Taken during the Tulip Week that took place two years ago. They were huge, gorgeous, and colourful. Spring is in the air!!! Ahh!	Vegas + other travels. Kev has been to the southern United States several times. Did some sound engineering thing in California and interned for Trent R. in New Orleans in, like, 2002. Spent a lot of time in the southern United States, SO anyways, he wants to visit New Orleans, Phoenix again (spent some time there, but I have a bad memory) and a bunch of places in the South. We're commiting to Vegas.
Female-authored text	Male-authored text

TABLE 11.5 ● Examples of Truthful and Deceptive Texts	
My best friend never gives me a hard time about anything. If we don't see each other or talk to each other for a while, it's not like anyone's mad. We could not see each other for years, and if we met up it would be like nothing happened. A lot of people in life can make you feel like you're being judged and most of the time make you feel that what you're doing isn't good enough. My best friend is one of the few people I don't feel that way around.	My best friend is very funny. He's always making jokes and making people laugh. We're such good friends because he can also be very serious when it comes to emotions and relationships. It keeps me from getting too relaxed and making a mistake like taking advantage of our friendship or not making an effort to keep it going. He's a pretty fragile person, and although it can be hard to keep him happy sometimes, it's all the more rewarding.
Truthful text	Deceptive text

Deception Detection

Yet another difficult task is that of identifying deceit in text (Mihalcea & Strapparava, 2009; Newman, Pennebaker, Berry, & Richards, 2003; Ott, Choi, Cardie, & Hancock, 2011). This has found applications not only in the legal domain but also in the detection of false reviews and deceptive posts on social media. As with author profiling, the linguistic clues that are most useful for the detection of deceit consist of function words (e.g., deceivers use self-referring expressions such as *I* or *we* less often); thus, humans have often very low performance at this task. Table 11.5 shows examples of truthful and deceptive texts.

Other Applications

Apart from the examples illustrated previously, there are many other applications of text classification. Some additional examples include the classification of texts by their language (e.g., English versus Chinese versus Romanian), the classification of the genre of a text (e.g., editorials versus movie reviews versus news), emotional content detection (e.g., happy versus sad versus angry), classification with respect to a specific dimension of the reader (e.g., interesting to me versus not interesting to me), and many others.

Representing Texts for Supervised Text Classification

Most text classification systems use a very high-dimensional feature space consisting of the words in the texts. That is, given a collection of texts, we can extract the *vocabulary* of that collection by identifying all the unique words. The words in the vocabulary will then constitute the feature space; therefore, each text in the collection will be represented as a vector in this space, using weights that represent the importance of a word in a given text.

Consider a simple example with just two texts: "Today is a beautiful day" and "Today is the day." The vocabulary consists of six words (*a, beautiful, day, is, the, today*); thus, the vectors used to represent these texts will all have a length of six. Assuming a very simple weight scheme, which just looks for the presence of a word in a text, the feature vector for the first text will be (1, 1, 1, 1, 0, 1) and for the second text will be (0, 0, 1, 1, 1, 1).

While individual words (also referred to as unigrams) are the most frequently used features for text classification, other features can also be used. For instance, one can use sequences of bigrams (two words at a time), trigrams, and so on. In the example just given, the vocabulary of bigrams would be *today_is, is_a, a_beautiful, beautiful_ day, is_the, the_day*, and the feature vectors for the two texts would be (1, 1, 1, 1, 0, 0) and (1, 0, 0, 0, 0, 1, 1). Of course, the higher the order of the n-grams used to generate the features, the sparser the representations will be.

In addition to word-based features, one can also use word classes to create features for text classification. There are many lexical resources that can be used as a source of word classes, such as WordNet, *Roget's Thesaurus*, or Linguistic Inquiry and Word Count (LIWC; see Chapter 4). In this representation, rather than use individual words, we use classes of words to create each feature. For instance, assuming the class of words *we*, including words such as *we, us, ourselves, our*, etc., and assuming a simple weighting scheme that uses the frequency of words, the value of this feature will be the total number of occurrences of *we* words inside the text. Using this technique of creating a cumulative weight for each word class, we can generate feature vectors that include one feature for each class—for example, 80 features if we use LIWC, 700 to 1,000 features if we use *Roget's*, etc.

Feature Weighting and Selection

Given the high-dimensional feature space typically used in text classification, feature weighting and feature selection play an important role. The question is this: How can we weight features so that we give higher weight to features that are more important for a given text than for others? Intuitively, we would like to give a low weight to words such as *is, a, have,* and *give* and a high weight to words such as *mining, classroom,* and *history*. Even among these last three words, if we think, for instance, about the topics discussed in this book, *history* and *classroom* should have lower weights than *mining*.

There are several ways to create feature weights. The simplest method is to use binary weights, which are either 0 or 1 depending on whether a word (or other n-gram) appears in a text or not. Another method is to use term frequency, which counts the number of occurrences of a word in a text. Yet another method is the so-called term frequency–inverse document frequency (tf.idf), which determines the term frequency of a word, as before, and then it divides it by the total number of texts where that word appears. Finally, a somewhat more advanced weighting method is information gain, which was presented in more detail in Chapter 6.

Text Classification Algorithms

Once texts are represented as feature vectors, they can be run through any supervised classification algorithm to automatically classify new incoming texts as belonging to one or more categories. Some of these algorithms will also produce a confidence measure associated with the classification, which will indicate the extent to which a certain test item can be accurately classified by the automatic categorizer.

The task of supervised learning was presented in Chapter 6, and many of the algorithms described in that chapter can be directly applied to the classification of texts. For instance, one can use SVMs or instance-based learning (see Chapter 6) to create learning models from the training instances, which can then be applied on the test instances. In this chapter, we present two classifiers that have been more widely used in conjunction with text classification.

Naive Bayes

Although Naive Bayes is one of the earliest algorithms for text classification, it is still one of the most widely used classification methods. Naive Bayes is based on the Bayes theorem from probability theory, which states the conditional probability of an event C given an event T.

$$P(C \mid T) = \frac{P(T \mid C)P(C)}{P(T)}$$

The Bayes theorem can be very easily inferred from the probability of joint events. The probability of C and T happening together can be written as $P(C,T) = P(C \mid T)P(T)$ or as $P(C,T) = P(T \mid C)P(C)$. The Bayes theorem follows directly from equating these two different ways of writing P(C,T).

Assuming the feature vector representation of a text T that we discussed before, let us say $\langle t_1, t_2, ..., t_n \rangle$ in text classification we want to find the category C_i in C such that it has the maximum probability given that text T. In other words, we want to find the category that satisfies

$C = \underset{C_i \in C}{\operatorname{argmax}} \ P(C_i \mid t_1, t_2, ..., t_n)$. Using the Bayes theorem, it follows that we want to find

$C = \underset{C_i \in C}{\operatorname{argmax}} \ \dfrac{P(t_1, t_2, ..., t_n \mid C_i)P(C_i)}{P(t_1, t_2, ..., t_n)}$. Given that the nominator is the same, regardless of the category C_i under consideration, we can rewrite this as

$C = \underset{C_i \in C}{\operatorname{argmax}}\ P(t_1, t_2, ..., t_n \mid C_i) P(c_i)$. An important assumption made in the Naive

Bayes algorithm (and the reason for the *naive* in its name) is the conditional independence of the features in a text representation. We assume that the features t_i inside a text are independent of each other, which allows us to rewrite the last equation as $C = \underset{C_i \in C}{\operatorname{argmax}}\ P(C_i) \underset{t_k \in T}{\prod} P(t_k \mid C_i)$. This final rewrite makes the algorithm

tractable and easily computable. We can compute $P(C_i)$ by counting the number of texts in the training data that are labeled with category C_i and dividing that by the total number of texts in the training data. We can compute $P(t_k|C_i)$ by counting the number of texts in the training data that are labeled with category C_i and include feature t_k, out of all the texts in the training data that are labeled with category

C_i: $P(C_i) = \dfrac{N(C = C_i)}{N}$ and $P(t_k \mid C_i) = \dfrac{N(T_k = t_k, C = C_i)}{N(C = C_i)}$

One final step that is often required is smoothing, which refers to the process of handling cases where there are no observations for a certain event (i.e., zero counts). To

address this, the last probability is often rewritten as $P(t_k \mid C_i) = \dfrac{N(T_k = t_k, C = C_i) + 1}{N(C = C_i) + k}$

where *k* is the size of the vocabulary (unique words) in the training data.

Rocchio Classifier

The Rocchio classifier builds upon the ideas of the vector-space model used in information retrieval (see Chapter 13), as it uses a measure of similarity between the representation of a test item and the representation of the training items.

In the training stage, the Rocchio classifier builds a prototype vector for each category in C: For each category, it identifies all the texts that are labeled with that category and adds up their feature vectors, thereby creating one feature vector also called the prototype vector for that category.

In the test stage, we calculate the similarity between the feature vector of the test text and each of the prototype vectors for the categories in C. As with the vector space model in information retrieval, multiple similarity measures can be used, with cosine similarity being the most widespread one. These similarity scores are then used to rank the categories with respect to their relevance to the test text.

Figure 11.2 shows a graphical illustration of the Rocchio classifier: The single-line arrows are the vector representations for the training documents in category C1, the double-line arrows are the vector representations for the training documents in category C2. From these vectors, the prototype vectors are built (the long single- or double-line arrows). The cosine similarity measures between the vector of the test text (the dashed arrow), which results in the selection of the category represented with a double line.

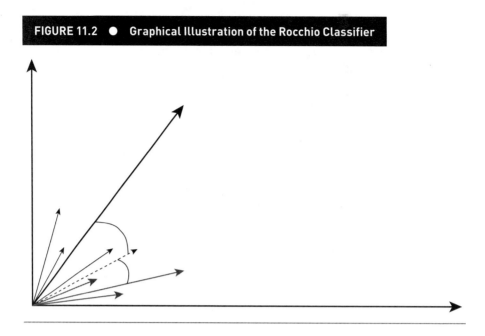

FIGURE 11.2 ● Graphical Illustration of the Rocchio Classifier

Bootstrapping in Text Classification

Another aspect of interest in automatic text classification is how to make effective use of raw textual data, which often comes at no cost. Assume, for instance, that we have 100 texts labeled for their topics, and we have 1,000,000 texts that are unlabeled. The question is how to make use of the unlabeled examples to improve the accuracy of a text classifier. There are several answers to this question, but the one that is often used in text classification is bootstrapping. This is a method where we train one or more classifiers on the existing training data and automatically label the raw texts. We then select the instances that are labeled with high confidence, move them to the training data set thus increasing its size, and then repeat the process of training and annotation. The training data set will therefore grow over time—and with it the accuracy of the system.

There are different ways of providing a confidence score for the classification. Among them, there is self-training, where a single classifier is used and the confidence score from the learning algorithm itself is used for the bootstrapping process. Another way is co-training, where two classifiers are used in combination and the agreement between the classifier is used as an indication of confidence. In this method, only instances where the two classifiers agree are selected for addition into the growing training set.

There are several issues that need to be addressed to apply bootstrapping in process. For instance, an important question is how many items to allow for addition into

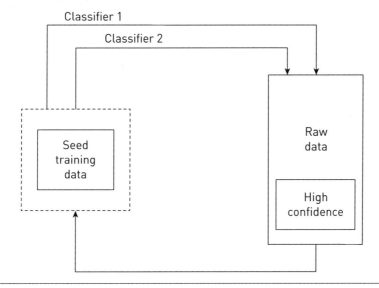

FIGURE 11.3   ●   Bootstrapping Text Classification

the training set in each iteration. Another question concerns the number of iterations that the classifier should run, as the general trend in bootstrapping is that the accuracy of the classifier(s) generally goes up for a few iterations, followed by a decrease due to the growing number of errors in the training data set.

Figure 11.3 illustrates the general bootstrapping process. Starting with a seed training data set, one or more classifiers are trained and used to identify items that can be confidently labeled inside a large, raw data set. Those items are added to the training data set, and the process is repeated for several iterations.

Evaluation of Text Classification

The methodology to evaluate text classification systems is the same as the evaluation used for general supervised learning methods. The reader is pointed to Chapter 6 to read about evaluation techniques and metrics and about learning curves.

Software and Data Sets for Text Classification

MALLET (MAchine Learning for LanguagE Toolkit; http://mallet.cs.umass.edu) is a collection of Java tools for statistical language processing, which also includes text classification and topic modeling. The AI::Categorizer (http://search.cpan.org/~kwil liams/AI-Categorizer-0.09/lib/AI/Categorizer.pm) is an easy-to-use Perl package for text

classification, which implements several classification algorithms. NLTK (http://www
.nltk.org) is a comprehensive toolkit for natural language processing, which also
includes software for text classification. The software packages for supervised learning
presented in Chapter 6 can also be used for text classification, after some preprocessing
steps that convert the input texts into feature vectors (see Chapter 6).

There are also several publicly available data sets that can be used to test text classification methods, including the Reuters news data set (https://kdd.ics.uci.edu/data
bases/reuters21578/reuters21578.html), deception data sets (http://web.eecs.umich
.edu/~mihalcea/downloads.html), language identification data sets (http://people.eng
.unimelb.edu.au/tbaldwin/#resources), and many others (https://archive.ics.uci.edu/
ml/datasets.html?format=&task=&att=&area=&numAtt=&numIns=&type=text&
sort=nameUp&view=table).

12

Information Extraction

Learning Objectives

The goals of Chapter 12 are to help readers do the following:

1. Understand the task of information extraction (IE) and its applications.
2. Learn about entity and relation extraction.
3. Learn about more advanced topics, such as web IE and template filling.

IE is the task of extracting structured information from unstructured data. The type of information to be extracted is usually predefined—for example, entities such as people or locations; events such as airline fare increases; or relations such as capitol-of relations between cities and countries. More recently, systems aiming at "open IE" (or web IE), where the information to be extracted is not predefined, have also started to gain attention.

Consider, for instance, the following text: "Virgin America CEO David Cush said Thursday that there will be 'continued fare wars' as American and Delta fight back against the discounters." There are several entities that can be identified—for example, organization names "Virgin America," "American," and "Delta"; people names "David Cush"; and a time entity "Thursday." We can also identify the CEO-of relation between "David Cush" and "Virgin America." An event is also described in the text "fight back against the discounters." As this example illustrates, there are several pieces of structured information that can be extracted from this unstructured text, including entities, events, and relations.

IE systems have many practical applications, which usually aim at organizing information in a way that is useful for further analysis tools or for people. IE systems can, for instance, be used to obtain names of diseases, symptoms, or drugs; companies and their CEOs; professor names and the universities where they teach; and so on.

In this chapter, we review the main directions of research focusing on the development of IE methods and tools. Specifically, we address in detail the topics of entity and relation extraction, we overview recent work in web IE, and also discuss the task of template filling that combines multiple information extractors together.

TABLE 12.1 ● Examples of Named Entities		
Type	**Category Examples**	**Examples**
PERSON	individuals, small groups	John Smith, Mrs. Jay
ORGANIZATION	companies, religious groups, political parties	Microsoft, Liberal Party
LOCATION	countries, cities, rivers	Romania, Washington D.C.

Entity Extraction

An important goal of IE is to identify instances of specific types in text, where a "type" could range from a person's name or a location, to all the entities that fall under a semantic category such as "animal" or "color," or to any specific events such as "rock concerts."

A well-defined and studied subclass of IE is named entity resolution, which aims to identify proper names that can be classified under a certain type. Common named entity resolution tasks are the recognition of persons, locations, and organizations, but there are also other more specialized tasks such as the recognition of composer names or computer science organizations. For instance, Table 12.1 shows examples of named entities along with their types.

One approach to named entity resolution is to first compile a set of representative seeds for the type to be identified in text—for example, Microsoft, Bloomberg, and Reuters are possible examples of organization names. Alternatively, and perhaps more commonly, one can start with a collection of texts manually annotated with the target named entity—for example, a collection of documents where all the organization names are explicitly labeled. A list of seeds can then be compiled from this labeled data set by extracting all the entities marked in the text. Given this starting point, one can locate the seeds inside new unannotated text and therefore learn rules that are good indicators of the presence of these seeds, such as "___ Inc." or "___ company" or "work at ___," which are patterns that are associated with the occurrence of organization names. These patterns, in turn, can be used to identify additional organization examples—for example, an occurrence such as "I work at Google" will identify Google as a new example of an organization, and it will be added to the list of organization names. The enlarged set of examples can once again be applied on text to learn new patterns, and so on. This is referred to as a bootstrapping process, where a list of organization names (or another named entity) and a list of patterns or rules to identify such organization names are incrementally learned from text. This process is similar to the one represented in Figure 11.3.

One danger with such bootstrapping methods is the infiltration of erroneous examples, which can lead to erroneous patterns, and consequently result in even more errors. The solution often used to address this is a scoring mechanism applied to both named entity examples and patterns, on a prelabeled collection. For instance, assuming the availability of a collection of texts previously labeled with all the named entities of interest, when learning a new pattern one can measure how many times that pattern correctly identifies the target named entities versus how many times that same pattern identifies other fragments of text. The patterns are then ranked in reverse order of their score, and only those that pass a certain threshold of "correctness" are allowed in the bootstrapping process.

Similar to this named entity resolution process, one can also build IE systems that learn semantic classes—for example, learn all the occurrences of "animals" or "colors" in a text (Riloff & Jones, 1999). Unlike named entity resolution, this IE task does not have some of the surface clues that named entities would have (e.g., spelling with an uppercase). Instead, the learning of semantic classes can benefit from the availability of reference works that include extensive word lists (e.g., WordNet or Roget, which include examples of animals, colors, and so on), which can be used as starting seeds for the bootstrapping process. Moreover, a similar bootstrapping approach can be used to identify events in text, such as "rock concerts."

An alternative approach for IE is to use machine learning to automatically classify whether a word is at the beginning of (B), inside (I), or outside (O) a piece of relevant information that is to be extracted. Once again, this approach presumes the availability of a collection of documents that have been previously annotated for the information to be extracted. For instance, given the text "I saw Mr. Jones at the market," and assuming we want to extract people names—that is, "Mr. Jones" in our example—the word *Mr.* will be labeled as B (i.e., it is at the beginning of the sequence "Mr. Jones"); the word *Jones* will be labeled as I; and all the other words will be labeled as O. With this formulation, we have a typical classification problem, where we need to assign a label to each word in a text. This classifier will implicitly learn the words that are often found inside relevant information (e.g., *Mr.*) and the words that are found in the immediate context (the patterns surrounding the relevant information). While in principle any machine learning algorithm could be used to perform this classification (see Chapter 6), the method that was generally found to work best is conditional random fields (McCallum & Li, 2003).

The evaluation of such entity extractors is often done by applying the IE system on a collection of texts that have been manually annotated for the entities of interest. On such a data set, one can measure the accuracy, precision, and recall of the system. For more information on these measures, see Chapter 13 on the evaluation of information retrieval systems, which can also be applied to IE.

Alternatively, when IE targets the extraction of semantic classes, which consist of finite even if large sets of words, one can use extensive listings of such words from existing resources (e.g., a listing of all the animals appearing in reference works such as WordNet or Roget), and perform accuracy, precision, and recall evaluations against these listings.

Relation Extraction

Entities are often connected by relations—for example, "company X is located in city Y," which reflects a "location" relation between X and Y, or "X is the sister of Y," which reflects a sibling relation between X and Y. The process of identifying these relation-ships between entities is called relation extraction, and it is another facet of IE.

The typical formulation of this problem assumes that two entities have been already identified, and the question is whether a certain relation holds between them. While the problem may seem simpler, as we mainly label a pair of entities as either yes (there is a relation) or no (there is not), in reality relation extraction is more difficult than entity extraction as it encompasses a larger number of factors that contribute to a decision.

Similar to entity extraction, a common approach to relation extraction is to first annotate a collection of documents with the relations of interest and then train a machine learning system to identify these relations. In addition to attributes that characterize each of the entities in the relation—for example, the tokens that are part of the entities, or their syntactic or semantic roles—there are also attributes that describe the connection between the entities, usually obtained by extracting the links from a syntactic parse tree or other graphical representation of the text. Given these attributes that model all the candidate pairs of entities (perhaps constrained by a max-imum acceptable distance between them)—some of which are connected by relations and some of which are not—a classifier can be trained to automatically determine if a relation exists between two given entities.

Web Information Extraction

The web has brought both challenges and opportunities for the task of IE. Importantly, the very large scale of web data is both an asset, in terms of providing large amounts of instances to train and bootstrap IE systems and in terms of providing data redun-dancy for quality verification, as well as a drawback as the web brings a significant amount of noise in the form of errors, ill-formed texts, heterogeneous formats, and so on.

There are several web scale IE systems that have been built to date. For the purpose of illustration, we will briefly describe two of them.

The first system is KnowItAll (Etzioni et al., 2004), which extracts facts and rela-tions from the web. The system is seeded with information obtained from an ontology, along with a few generic templates, which it then uses to create text extraction rules. For instance, the general template "NounPhrase1 such as NounPhraseList" can be applied on text together with some seeds such as Paris and London are cities to infer a generic syntactic pattern of the form "cities such as <?>" that can be used to extract additional city names. Note that the template rules are generic and domain indepen-dent and therefore can be automatically instantiated for the extraction of various entities (e.g., cities, countries, colors). Queries formed from its text extraction rules are run against a search engine, and the information obtained is validated by a statistical module in KnowItAll that assesses the correctness likelihood for the each piece of IE. The information is then stored in a database for further analysis. While the initial ver-sion of KnowItAll included a little over 50,000 facts, follow-ups such as ReVerb (Fader, Soderland, & Etzioni, 2011) and TextRunner (Banko, Cafarella, Soderland, Broadhead,

& Etzioni, 2007) had significantly larger coverage including more than 3 million entities and 600,000 relation extractions, among other knowledge pieces.

The second web system is NELL (Never-Ending Language Learning; Carlson et al., 2010), which is another open IE system that creates candidate "beliefs" by processing a very large number of webpages, and it then automatically assesses the confidence of these beliefs before committing them to a database. A characteristic of NELL is that it uses bootstrapping to improve its own performance over time, by using information it learned to build even more accurate information extractors. Examples of relations learned by NELL are "WWCS is a radio station" or "haori is a kind of clothing." At the time of this writing, the system has accumulated close to 50 million facts, out of which it has high confidence in almost 3 million facts.

Template Filling

There are many situations when the pieces of information being extracted are related to one another in that they represent different aspects of the same type of situation or event. For instance, if we speak about a terrorist attack, relevant information would consist of location of the attack, the date and time of the attack, the group behind the attack, the number of victims, and so on. These aspects of an event are often referred to as slots, and they form a template for that event. The process of finding the values for each of the slots is called slot filling, and the overall process of filling in the values for all the aspects in a template is called template filling.

In most cases, separate IE algorithms can be trained following the same set of steps as outlined before: One first annotates a set of documents with the information of interest (i.e., each of the slots marked explicitly in text) or identifies a set of seed values for each slot. A classifier is then trained to recognize patterns that are associated with these slot occurrences, finally followed by a boostrapping process that automatically grows the lists of patterns and possible values for each slot.

Recent work has also considered the joint application of the IE algorithms for the individual slots, with the idea that there might be some dependencies between the slots. For instance, the location of terrorist attacks might have some association with the groups behind the attacks, and so forth. This is referred to as joint aspect learning, or joint slot filling (Mukherjee & Liu, 2012).

Software and Data Sets for Information Extraction and Text Mining

While IE is often domain specific—and therefore researchers or users of IE systems often prefer to build their own IE tools—there are a few IE systems available that can be used as a starting point. For instance, GATE (https://gate.ac.uk) from the University of Sheffield includes an IE component. Different versions of web IE are also available (http://reverb.cs.washington.edu and http://openie.allenai.org), which are implementations of open IE. Also worth mentioning is the DeepDive (http://deepdive.stanford .edu) open source system that extracts entities and relations from unstructured input.

13

Information Retrieval

Learning Objectives

The goals of Chapter 13 are to help readers do the following:

1. Understand the foundations of information retrieval (IR), including the main components of an IR system and the main IR models.
2. Learn about the vector space model, which is the most widely used IR method.
3. Learn about evaluation methodologies in IR.
4. Understand the main aspects of web-based IR.

I R systems do the following:

[They] process files of records and requests for information, and identify and retrieve from the files certain records in response to the information requests. The retrieval of particular records depends on the similarity between the records and the queries, which in turn is measured by comparing the values of certain attributes to records and information requests.

This is the definition that Gerald Salton, the founder of the IR field, provided back in 1989 (Salton, 1989), and while the field has come a long way since its inception in the 1980s, the core goals remain the same: to process requests for information and to identify and retrieve relevant information in response to these requests.

Thus, the main goals of an IR system are to (1) *index* data—that is, organize the data in such a way that it can be easily retrieved later on—and (2) *retrieve* data—that is, take information requests in the form of queries and return relevant documents. IR systems are generally concerned not only with retrieving relevant information but also with being able to efficiently handle very large data collections.

IR systems find applications in many different areas, including web searches, which is perhaps the most widely used IR application; searches in library records; searches for other media, such as images or music; searches across languages where the information request is in one language and the data being searched is in another; vertical searches, including e-mails, patents, and forums; and many others. IR systems are often applied on unstructured textual documents, although they can also be applied on images, sounds, and videos and can be used to identify relevant information from structured databases.

In this chapter we first review the theoretical foundations of IR, followed by a presentation of the main components of an IR system and a description of the three main IR models. We then present in more detail the vector space model and discuss the evaluation methodologies used to assess the quality of IR systems. We also address the task of web-based IR methods and highlight their differences with respect to traditional IR methods.

Theoretical Foundations

An essential concept in IR is that of *relevance*. Given an input query that is being run against an IR system, the relevance of a document returned by the system in response to this query is highly subjective. First, it depends on whether it is on the proper subject: Does the document address the topic of the query? Second, it also matters if the information in the document is timely: If a query asks about the president of the United States, a document that refers to the current president will be considered relevant, whereas the document referring to previous presidencies will not be relevant. Third, the authority of the source of the document is also very important; we oftentimes find conflicting or even deceptive data on the web, and the most trustworthy sources should be prioritized as being more relevant. In general, when judging relevancy, the main criterion is whether the documents being returned satisfy the information needs of the user.

The simplest IR system that models this notion of relevance is one that looks for the query inside the documents. Since the exact query is often unlikely to appear in any document, a more relaxed and more frequently used IR model is one that looks for the query words inside the document in any order. This is called a *bag-of-words* approach. On top of this representation, there are several IR models that can be used, such as the Boolean model, which looks for occurrences of key words from the query inside the document; the vector space model, which calculates a similarity between the bag-of-words representations of a document and of the query; or the probabilistic model, which determines the likelihood of a document to be relevant to a certain query using probabilities over key words.

Components of an Information Retrieval System

As mentioned before, the two main functionalities of an IR system are to index and retrieve data. In addition, an IR system also generally performs a number of other

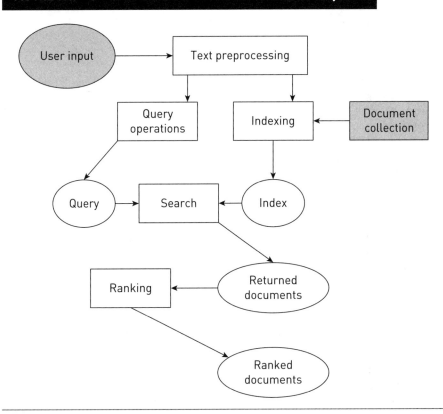

FIGURE 13.1 ● **Architecture of an Information Retrieval System**

functions, such as preprocessing the documents and the queries and ranking documents. The diagram of a typical IR system is shown in Figure 13.1.

As seen in the diagram, an IR system performs the following operations:

Text preprocessing. This includes operations such as tokenization, stop word removal, and stemming (see Chapter 5).

Indexing. This module takes as input a set of documents and constructs an inverted index, which is a data structure that maps words to documents by indicating for each word in which document it can be found. The inverted index has to be an efficient search structure so that the retrieval of information for every word in the index is very efficient.

Search. This module takes as input a token from the query and searches the inverted index for the corresponding entry. It returns the list of documents that contain that token, along with additional information such as token weights.

Ranking. This is the component that scores all the documents returned by the search module according to a relevance metric. The documents are then sorted in reversed order of their scores so that the most relevant documents are returned first.

User interface. This module takes care of the interaction between the user and the IR system. It performs functions such as getting the query from the user, returning documents from the search and ranking, or visualizing the results. The user interface also performs query operations, which consist of processes such as spelling correction, expansion of query words with synonyms from a thesaurus, and query transformation using relevance feedback.

Information Retrieval Models

There are several IR models that have been proposed and implemented over time. The three main ones are the Boolean model, the vector space model, and the probabilistic model.

The Boolean model is one of the first IR models. It is based on set theory, and it uses Boolean logic using operators such as AND, OR, and NOT that connect the query tokens. For example, the query *social AND sciences* will return only documents that contain both terms *social* and *sciences*. Conversely, *social OR sciences* will return documents that include at least one of the terms. Figure 13.2 shows three examples of Boolean queries and the documents they return, using a Venn diagram, where a circle labeled with the term T corresponds to all the documents that contain T.

There are several extensions of the Boolean model, including the fuzzy IR model, which allows for a partial matching between tokens (e.g., *orange* will not match *computer,* but *orange* will partially match *fruit*), and the extended Boolean model, which calculates a matching score between the query and the documents, similar to the vector space model discussed next.

FIGURE 13.2 ● Examples of Boolean Queries

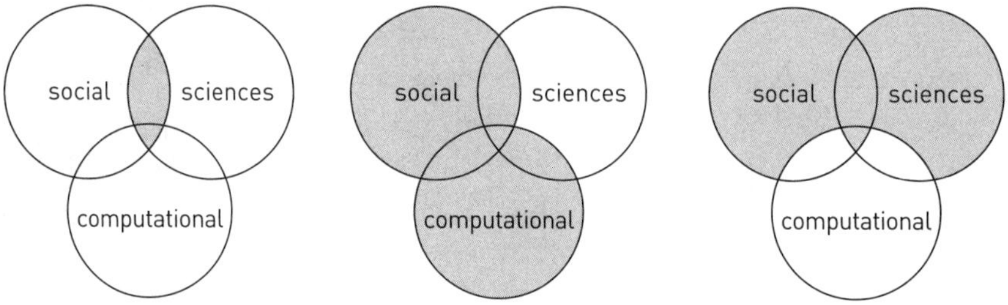

a. social AND sciences

b. social OR computational

c. (social AND sciences) OR NOT computational

The vector space model was introduced by Gerald Salton in 1983 (Salton & McGill, 1986) and is the most popular IR model. Today's search engines also rely on the vector space model as one of their core components. The model uses a vector representation of queries and documents in a high-dimensional space where each term in the vocabulary corresponds to one dimension. Each token inside the vectors is weighted; these vector representations are used to calculate the degree of similarity between a query and a document; and these similarity scores are used to rank the documents. Since it is the most widely used IR model, we describe it in more detail in a separate section.

Extensions of the vector space model include latent semantic analysis (LSA; Landauer, Foltz, & Laham, 1998), which maps the term *vector space* into a lower dimensional space through singular value decomposition (SVD; Golub & Reinsch, 1970) and replaces the indexes that use sets of terms with indexes that use latent concepts (see also Chapter 10). Another extension is explicit semantic analysis (ESA; Egozi, Markovitch, & Gabrilovich, 2011), which creates a vector representation for each word in the vocabulary by using a vector that consists of the frequencies of the word inside each Wikipedia article. These word vectors are added up to generate vectors for the query and the documents, which are then used to calculate the degree of similarity between the query and each document.

The probabilistic model (Maron & Kuhns, 1960; Robertson & Sparck Jones, 1976) relies on probability theory and models the likelihood of a document to be relevant. One way to think about the IR problem in a probabilistic framework is to imagine that given a query, there is an ideal set of documents. The probabilistic model attempts to identify this ideal set by learning probabilities associated with words inside relevant documents. The model works iteratively, where the user inspects an initial set of documents identified by the system (e.g., by using a simple Boolean model) and provides feedback regarding the relevance of the documents in this set. The IR system uses this information to learn the probability of individual words to belong to relevant (or irrelevant) documents and relies on these probabilities to identify additional relevant documents.

Consider, for instance, an example where we have a collection of documents—some of which contain a specific term *T*. A user will mark a subset of the documents retrieved in the initial iteration of a search as being relevant; a fraction of these relevant documents identified by the user will include, among others, the term *T*. We can therefore use a probabilistic formulation to determine how important is the term *T* to this search by calculating the probability that *T* belongs to a relevant document, defined as the total number of relevant documents that contain *T* divided by the total number of relevant documents. In a similar fashion, we can also calculate the probability of nonrelevance for *T*, which is the total number of nonrelevant documents that contain *T* divided by the nonrelevant documents that do not contain *T*. We can then calculate a score for *T* that divides its probability of relevance by its probability of nonrelevance. For each document in the collection, we then identify those terms that overlap with the query and add up their probabilistic scores for a document score that can be used to generate a ranking over documents.

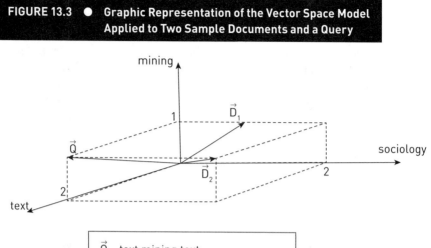

FIGURE 13.3 ● Graphic Representation of the Vector Space Model Applied to Two Sample Documents and a Query

$\vec{Q}$ = text mining text

$\vec{D}_1$ = mining sociology

$\vec{D}_2$ = text sociology mining sociology

The Vector Space Model

As briefly mentioned before, the vector space model uses a vector representation in a high-dimensional space for both queries and documents. This space consists of one dimension for each term in the vocabulary of the collection, and correspondingly, the vectors will reflect the presence or absence of vocabulary terms in the query or the documents.

As an example, consider the graphic illustration from Figure 13.3. In this simple case, the vocabulary includes three words: *text*, *mining*, and *sociology*; therefore, we use a three-dimensional space, with one dimension for each of the three words. Queries and documents will then be represented as vectors in this space. For instance, the query "text mining text" includes two occurrences of the word text and one occurrence of mining, and thus the vector for this query is $\vec{Q}$ = (2, 1, 0), where 2 is the weight for the word text, 1 is the weight for mining, and 0 is the weight for sociology. Similarly, the vector for $\vec{D}_1$ is $\vec{D}_1$ = (0, 1, 1) and for $\vec{D}_2$ is $\vec{D}_2$ = (1, 1, 2). Next, we can build upon these representations and measure the similarity between the query vector and the document vectors, which will result in a ranking over the documents.

There are several ways to measure the similarity of two vectors. The most commonly used one in IR is cosine similarity, defined as the following:

$$sim(\vec{Q}, \vec{D}_1) = \frac{\vec{Q}.\vec{D}}{|\vec{Q}||\vec{D}_1|} = \frac{\sum\limits_{i=1}^{V} t_{i\vec{Q}} t_{i\vec{D}_1}}{\sqrt{\sum\limits_{i=1}^{V} t_{i\vec{Q}}^2} \sqrt{\sum\limits_{i=1}^{V} t_{i\vec{D}_1}^2}}$$ Given a query and a document, this calcu-

lates the sum of the products of the weights of the corresponding terms in the vector representations (also called inner product) and divides that with the product of the lengths of the query and the document.

Using the example from Figure 13.3, with $\vec{Q} = (2,1,0)$ and $\vec{D}_1 = (0,1,1)$, the inner product of $\vec{Q}$ and $\vec{D}_1$ is 2x0+1x0+1x1 = 1, the length of the query is $\sqrt{2^2 + 1^2 + 0^2} = 2.23$ and the length of $\vec{D}_1$ is $\sqrt{0^2 + 1^2 + 1^2} = 1.41$, and thus the cosine similarity between $\vec{Q}$ and $\vec{D}_1$ is 0.31.

An important component of the vector space model is the weighting scheme used for the terms in the vocabulary. The simplest weights that one can use are the number of occurrences of the terms, as done in the previously given example, where the weight for "text" inside $\vec{Q}$ was set to 2. This turns out not to work very well in practice, as common words such as *the* or *of* will end up having a very large weight. Instead, the weighting scheme used by most IR systems is referred to as tf.idf (term frequency–inverse document frequency), and for each term it calculates the total number of occurrences inside a document divided by the total number of documents in the collection that contain that term. The actual formula used for this weighting is as follows:

$$t_{ij} = \text{tf}_{ij} \times \log_{10}(N / \text{df}_i)$$

Here, t_{ij} refers to the weight of term t_i inside document j; tf_{ij} refers to the term frequency of that term inside document j; N is the total number of documents in the collection; and df_i is the total number of documents that contain term t_i. For instance, if a word occurs two times inside a document, and there are 1,000 total documents in the collection out of which 50 contain that word, its weight is $2 \log_{10}(1000/50) = 2.60$.

Since document collections tend to get very large, the practical implementation of the vector space model includes the following steps:

1. Preprocess all the documents and queries (tokenization, stop word removal, etc.).
2. Loop through all the terms in the documents, and create an inverted index that maps each term to a list of documents that contain that term.
3. Calculate tf.idf weightings for all the terms in the documents and queries.
4. Given a query, use the inverted index to identify the documents that contain terms from the query.
5. Measure the cosine similarity between the query and each of the documents identified at step 4.
6. Rank the documents in reverse order of their cosine similarity.

Evaluation of Information Retrieval Models

As with any other automatic system, an important question in IR is how to evaluate the quality of a retrieval model. There are several aspects that matter, including whether the system satisfies the user's information need and how fast the system indexes and retrieves documents. Moreover, system development raises questions concerning the performance of individual components—for example, whether stop words should be removed or not and what ranking method to use, which are also best answered via system evaluations.

The standard methodology for evaluating IR systems is to create a gold standard collection against which one can measure the performance of the system. These collections usually include a set of documents and a set of queries, along with manual relevance judgments consisting of binary assessments of either "relevant" or "nonrelevant" for each query and each document.

Given such a collection, for every query, the set of documents can be split into four different categories, as shown in Figure 13.4. On this matrix, we can define the most frequently used evaluation measures in IR, namely *precision* and *recall*. Precision is defined as the total number of relevant documents retrieved divided by the total number of retrieved documents ($x/(x+z)$). Recall is defined as the total number of relevant documents retrieved, divided by the total number of relevant documents ($x/(x+y)$). These two evaluation metrics are complementary in that they measure two different aspects of the IR system: Precision measures the ability of the system to top rank the documents that are most relevant, whereas recall measures the ability of the system to find all the relevant documents in the collection. Precision and recall vary inversely and are often reported using a precision-recall curve, which shows the precision of the system for varying levels of recall (e.g., what is the precision of the

FIGURE 13.4 ● Division of Documents in a Collection With Respect to a Query

	Retrieved	Not
Relevant	**x**	**y**
Irrelevant	**z**	**w**

system when the recall is 0.3). They can also be combined into one single measure, called the F-measure, which is the harmonic mean of precision and recall:

$$F\text{-}measure = \frac{2 \times Precision \times Recall}{Precision + Recall}$$

In addition to precision, recall, and F-measure, there are several other evaluation metrics, such as R-precision (which calculates the precision of the IR system when the total number of documents returned by the system is equal to the total number of relevant documents in the collection); precision@K (which is the precision of the system for the top K returned documents); mean average precision (which is the average of the precision@K metric for each of the top K documents), and so on.

Web-Based Information Retrieval

IR systems were originally used for retrieving information from offline collections such as library records and collections of scientific papers. But for the past two decades, the most frequent application of IR has been web searches. There are two important differences between traditional IR and web-based IR. First, the collection of documents used in web-based IR is not available as a static, offline collection but rather is dynamic and has to be periodically crawled from the web (see Chapter 3). There are many challenges that come with the compilation of document collections from the web, including the dynamic nature of the documents (new documents appear all the time, and existing documents are either changed or permanently removed), the volume of the data (there are tens of billions of pages on the web, and their number is continuously growing), the heterogeneity of the documents (e.g., different media types including text, images, videos, different languages, and different character sets), and the quality of the data (there is no uniform structure used in the documents, there are many HTML and language errors, and there is no control of the trustworthiness of web-based information). Search engines often put significant effort into the process of compiling comprehensive and clean collections of webpages that are used for web searches.

The second important difference between traditional and web-based IR concerns the availability of links between the documents in the collection. Links enable the use of link-based retrieval algorithms in addition to content-based retrieval (e.g., the vector space model). PageRank (Page, Brin, Motwani, & Winograd, 1999) is a famous example of link-based analysis for web searches, introduced as a method for ranking the importance of webpages as part of the Google search engine. PageRank is a graph centrality algorithm. It is essentially a way of deciding the importance of a webpage within the web graph based on global information recursively drawn from the entire graph.

The basic idea implemented by the PageRank model is that of "voting" or "recommendation." When one webpage links to another one, it is basically casting a vote for that other page. The higher the number of votes that are cast for a page, the higher the importance of the page. Moreover, the importance of the page casting the vote determines how important the vote itself is, and this information is also taken into account in the ranking model. Hence, the score associated with a webpage is calculated based on the votes that are cast for it and the scores of the vertices casting these votes.

Formally, let G = (V, E) be a directed graph with the set of vertices *V* and set of edges *E*, where *E* is a subset of V × V. For a given vertex V_i, let $In(V_i)$ be the set of vertices that point to it (predecessors), and let $Out(V_i)$ be the set of vertices that vertex V_i points to (successors). The PageRank score of a vertex V_i is defined as follows (Page et al., 1999):

$$S(V_i) = \frac{(1-d)}{|V|} + d * \sum_{j \in In(V_i)} \frac{1}{|Out(V_j)|} S(V_j)$$

Eq. 13.1

Here, *d* is a damping factor that can be set between 0 and 1, which has the role of integrating into the model the probability of jumping from a given vertex to another random vertex in the graph. The factor *d* is usually set to 0.85 (Page et al., 1999).

To illustrate the working of the PageRank algorithm, consider the graph in Figure 13.5, and assume each vertex is assigned with an initial value of 0.25. The PageRank score can then be calculated by using formula 13.1. Running the algorithm for 10 iterations leads to the scores shown in Table 13.1.

After running the algorithm through convergence, a score is associated with each vertex, which represents the "importance" of the vertex within the graph. Note that the final values obtained after PageRank runs to completion are not affected by the choice of the initial values; only the number of iterations to convergence may be different.

The evaluation of web-based IR is also somewhat different compared to traditional IR systems. On the web, given the large number of documents that are being searched, it is impossible to measure the recall of an IR system. Instead, a technique called pooling is used to sample the collection and select random documents from the set of documents that have at least one word in common with the query. Relevance judgment is then performed on these documents, and the recall of the IR system is measured with respect to this sample collection. The precision of web IR systems is often

FIGURE 13.5 ●   A Sample Web Graph

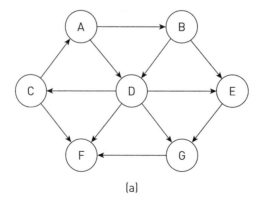

(a)

TABLE 13.1 ● Output of the PageRank Algorithm Run on the Directed Graph From Figure 13.3							
Iteration	A	B	C	D	E	F	G
1	0.250	0.250	0.250	0.250	0.250	0.250	0.250
2	0.128	0.128	0.075	0.234	0.181	0.393	0.075
3	0.053	0.076	0.071	0.130	0.125	0.166	0.071
4	0.052	0.044	0.049	0.076	0.081	0.140	0.049
5	0.042	0.043	0.038	0.062	0.056	0.100	0.038
6	0.037	0.039	0.035	0.058	0.053	0.083	0.035
7	0.036	0.037	0.034	0.054	0.050	0.078	0.034
8	0.036	0.037	0.033	0.053	0.049	0.076	0.033
9	0.035	0.037	0.033	0.052	0.048	0.075	0.033
10	0.035	0.036	0.033	0.052	0.048	0.074	0.033

measured on the top 10 documents returned by the system, as it has been found that web users rarely look for documents beyond the first page of results returned by the search engine. A benefit that comes with the linked nature of web documents is the possibility of using "click-through" information as a way to evaluate the relevance of a document: Users click on the links to a webpage returned for a search query if they believe that page is likely to be relevant based on the snippet presented by the search engine. This "click" is recorded and later used by the web IR system as a way to estimate the relevance of that one webpage for the given search query. Finally, it is also worth mentioning the A/B testing technique that search engines use to evaluate changes in the IR system (including changes in its user interface). Given a certain version of the web IR system and given a change that is being tested, a small (typically less than 1%) fraction of the users is sent to the variant of the system that implements the change, while the remaining users continue to use the original version of the system. Click-through data is then used to evaluate the usefulness of the change.

Software and Data Sets for Information Retrieval

Two of the most popular information retrieval systems are Solr (http:// lucene.apache .org/solr) and Indri (http://www.lemurproject.org/indri.php), which implement efficient text search for very large collections. Also popular is Lucene (http://lucene.apache.org), which is the precursor of Solr.

There are many data sets that are publicly available and widely used in IR evaluations, including those available through the Text REtrieval Conference (http://trec.nist .gov) or through its European counterpart CLEF (http://www.clef-initiative.eu).

14

Sentiment Analysis

Learning Objectives

The goals of Chapter 14 are to help readers do the following:

1. Understand the tasks of subjectivity and sentiment analysis and the applications where they may be useful.
2. Learn about resources for subjectivity and sentiment analysis, specifically addressing lexicons and corpora.
3. Learn about tools for subjectivity and sentiment analysis that rely on these resources.

S ubjectivity and sentiment analysis focuses on the automatic identification of private states, such as opinions, emotions, sentiments, evaluations, beliefs, and speculations in natural language. While subjectivity classification labels text as either subjective or objective, sentiment classification adds an additional level of granularity, by further classifying subjective text as either positive, negative, or neutral.

To date, a large number of text processing applications have already used techniques for automatic sentiment and subjectivity analysis, including automatic expressive text-to-speech synthesis (Alm, Roth, & Sproat, 2005), tracking sentiment timelines in online forums and news (Balog, Mishne, & de Rijke, 2005; Lloyd, Kechagias, & Skiena, 2005), customer relationship management (Kim & Hovy, 2006), and mining opinions from product reviews (Hu & Liu, 2004). In many natural language processing tasks, subjectivity and sentiment classification have been used as a first phase filtering to generate more viable data. Research that benefited from this additional layering ranges from question answering (Yu & Hatzivassiloglou, 2003) to conversation summarization (Carenini, Ng, & Zhou, 2007) and text semantic analysis (Esuli & Sebastiani, 2006a; Wiebe & Mihalcea, 2006).

Much of the research work to date on sentiment and subjectivity analysis has been applied to English, but work on other languages is growing, including Japanese (Takamura, Inui, & Okumura, 2006), Chinese (Zagibalov & Carroll, 2008), German (Kim & Hovy, 2006), and Romanian (Mihalcea, Banea, & Wiebe, 2007).

In this chapter, we review the main directions of research, focusing on the development of resources and tools for subjectivity and sentiment analysis.

Specifically, we identify and overview two main types of resources: (1) lexicons, which consist of extensive listings of words and phrases annotated with a subjectivity, sentiment, and/or emotion label, and (2) corpora, which are collections of sentences or short documents labeled for subjectivity or sentiment. We also describe the methods most frequently used to automatically identify the subjectivity or sentiment of a text, by relying on various resources used in an unsupervised or a supervised framework.

Theoretical Foundations

An important kind of information that is conveyed in many types of written and spoken discourse is the mental or emotional state of the writer or speaker or some other entity referenced in the discourse. News articles, for example, often report emotional responses to a story in addition to the facts. Editorials, reviews, weblogs, and political speeches convey the opinions, beliefs, or intentions of the writer or speaker. A student engaged in a tutoring session may express his or her understanding or uncertainty.

Quirk et al. (1985) give us a general term, *private state*, for referring to these mental and emotional states. In their words, a private state is a state that is not open to objective observation or verification: "A person may be observed to assert that God exists, but not to believe that God exists. Belief is in this sense 'private'" (Quirk et al., 1985). A term for the linguistic expression of private states, adapted from literary theory (Banfield, 1982), is *subjectivity. Subjectivity analysis* is the task of identifying when a private state is being expressed and identifying attributes of the private state. Attributes of private states include who is expressing the private state, the type(s) of attitude being expressed, about whom or what the private state is being expressed, the polarity of the private state (i.e., whether it is positive or negative), and so on. For example, consider the following sentence: The choice of Miers was praised by the Senate's top Democrat, Harry Reid of Nevada.

In this sentence, the phrase "was praised by" indicates that a private state is being expressed. The private state, according to the writer of the sentence, is being expressed by Reid, and it is about the choice of Miers, who was nominated to the Supreme Court by President Bush in October 2005. The type of the attitude is a sentiment (an evaluation, emotion, or judgment), and the polarity is positive (Wilson, 2008).

This chapter is primarily concerned with detecting the presence of subjectivity and, further, identifying its polarity. These judgments may be made along several dimensions. One dimension is context. On the one hand, we may judge the subjectivity and polarity of words, out of context: *Love* is subjective and positive, while *hate* is subjective and *negative*. At the other extreme, we have "full" contextual interpretation of language as it is being used in a text or dialogue. In fact, there is a continuum from one to the other, and we can define several natural language processing tasks along this continuum. The first is developing a word-level subjectivity lexicon, a list of key words that have been gathered together because they have subjective usages; polarity information is often added to such lexicons. In addition to *love* and *hate*, other examples are *brilliant* and *interest* (positive polarity) as well as *alarm* (negative polarity).

We can also classify word *senses* according to their subjectivity and polarity. Consider, for example, the following two senses of *interest* from WordNet (Miller, 1995):

Interest, involvement—(a sense of concern with and curiosity about someone or something; "an interest in music")

Interest—a fixed charge for borrowing money; usually a percentage of the amount borrowed; "how much interest do you pay on your mortgage?"

The first sense is subjective, with positive polarity. But the second sense is not (nonsubjective senses are called *objective* senses)—it does not refer to a private state.

Word- and sense-level subjectivity lexicons are important because they are useful resources for *contextual subjectivity analysis* (Wilson, 2008)—recognizing and extracting private state expressions in an actual text or dialogue. We can judge the subjectivity and polarity of texts at several different levels. At the document level, we can ask if a text is opinionated and, if so, whether it is mainly positive or negative. We can perform more fine-grained analysis and ask if a sentence contains any subjectivity. For instance, consider the following examples from Wilson (2008). The first sentence that follows is subjective (and has positive polarity), but the second one is objective, because it does not contain any subjective expressions:

He spins a riveting plot that grabs and holds the reader's interest.

The notes do not pay interest.

Even further, individual expressions may be judged—for example, that *spins*, *riveting*, and *interest* in the first sentence above are subjective expressions. A more interesting example appears in this sentence: "Cheers to Timothy Whitfield for the wonderfully horrid visuals." While *horrid* would be listed as having negative polarity in a word-level subjectivity lexicon, in this context, it is being used positively: *wonderfully horrid* expresses a positive sentiment toward the visuals (similarly, *cheers* expresses a positive sentiment toward *Timothy Whitfield*).

Lexicons

One of the most frequently used lexicons is perhaps the subjectivity and sentiment lexicon provided with the OpinionFinder distribution (Wiebe, Wilson, & Cardie, 2005).

The lexicon was compiled from manually developed resources augmented with entries learned from corpora. It contains 6,856 unique entries, out of which 990 are multiword expressions. The entries in the lexicon have been labeled for part of speech as well as for reliability—those that appear most often in subjective contexts are *strong* clues of subjectivity, while those that appear less often, but still more often than expected by chance, are labeled *weak*. Each entry is also associated with a polarity label, indicating whether the corresponding word or phrase is positive, negative, or neutral. To illustrate, consider the following entry from the OpinionFinder lexicon: *type = strongsubj word1 = agree pos1 = verb mpqapolarity = weakpos*, which indicates that the word *agree* when used as a *verb* is a strong clue of subjectivity and has a polarity that is weakly positive.

Another lexicon that has been often used in polarity analysis is the General Inquirer (Stone, 1968). It is a dictionary of about 10,000 words grouped into about 180 categories, which have been widely used for content analysis. It includes semantic classes (e.g., animate, human), verb classes (e.g., negatives, becoming verbs), cognitive orientation classes (e.g., causal, knowing, perception), and others. Two of the largest categories in the General Inquirer are the valence classes, which form a lexicon of 1,915 positive words and 2,291 negative words.

SentiWordNet (Esuli & Sebastiani, 2006b) is a resource for opinion mining built on top of WordNet, which assigns each synset in WordNet with a score triplet (positive, negative, and objective), indicating the strength of each of these three properties for the words in the synset. The SentiWordNet annotations were automatically generated, starting with a set of manually labeled synsets. Currently, SentiWordNet includes an automatic annotation for all the synsets in WordNet, totaling more than 100,000 words.

Corpora

Subjectivity and sentiment annotated corpora are useful not only as a means to train automatic classifiers but also as resources to extract opinion mining lexicons. For instance, a large number of the entries in the OpinionFinder lexicon mentioned in the previous section were derived based on a large opinion-annotated corpus.

The MPQA corpus (Wiebe et al., 2005) was collected and annotated as part of a 2002 workshop on multiperspective question answering (thus, the MPQA acronym). It is a collection of 535 English-language news articles from a variety of news sources manually annotated for opinions and other private states (i.e., beliefs, emotions, sentiments, speculations). The corpus was originally annotated at clause and phrase level, but sentence-level annotations associated with the data set can also be derived via simple heuristics (Wiebe et al., 2005).

Another manually annotated corpus is the collection of newspaper headlines created and used during the recent SemEval task on "Affective Text'" (Strapparava & Mihalcea, 2007). The data set consists of 1,000 test headlines and 200 development headlines, each of them annotated with the six Eckman emotions (anger, disgust, fear, joy, sadness, surprise) and their polarity orientation (positive, negative).

Two other data sets, both of them covering the domain of movie reviews, are a polarity data set consisting of 1,000 positive and 1,000 negative reviews, and a subjectivity data set consisting of 5,000 subjective and 5,000 objective sentences. Both data sets have been introduced in Pang and Lee (2004) and have been used to train opinion mining classifiers. Given the domain-specificity of these collections, they were found to lead to accurate classifiers for data belonging to the same or similar domains. More recently, a much larger movie review data set has been introduced (Maas et al., 2011), consisting of 50,000 full-length reviews collected from the IMDb website.

Research in sentiment analysis has also benefited from the growing number of product reviews available online, on sites such as Amazon.com or epinions.com, which can be used to build very large sentiment annotated data sets (Hu & Liu, 2004). Such reviews are usually available in many languages, thus enabling the construction of sentiment analysis tools in languages other than English (Nakagawa, Inui, & Kurohashi, 2010).

Tools

There are a large number of approaches that have been developed to date for sentiment and subjectivity analysis in English. The methods can be roughly classified into two categories: (1) rule-based systems, relying on manually or semiautomatically constructed lexicons, and (2) machine learning classifiers, trained on opinion-annotated corpora.

Among the rule-based systems, one of the most frequently used is OpinionFinder (Wiebe et al., 2005), which automatically annotates the subjectivity of new text based on the presence (or absence) of words or phrases in a large lexicon.

Briefly, the OpinionFinder high-precision classifier relies on three main heuristics to label subjective and objective sentences: (1) if two or more strong subjective expressions occur in the same sentence, the sentence is labeled *subjective*; (2) if no strong subjective expressions occur in a sentence, and at most two weak subjective expressions occur in the previous, current, and next sentence combined, then the sentence is labeled *objective*; and (3) if the previous rules do not apply, the sentence is labeled *unknown*. The classifier uses the clues from a subjectivity lexicon and the rules mentioned previously to harvest subjective and objective sentences from a large amount of unannotated text; this data is then used to automatically identify a set of extraction patterns, which are then used iteratively to identify a larger set of subjective and objective sentences. In addition to the high-precision classifier, OpinionFinder also includes a high-coverage classifier. This high-precision classifier is used to automatically produce an English labeled data set, which can then be used to train a high-coverage subjectivity classifier. When evaluated on the MPQA corpus, the high-precision classifier was found to lead to a precision of 86.7% and a recall of 32.6%, whereas the high-coverage classifier has a precision of 79.4% and a recall of 70.6%.

Another unsupervised system worth mentioning, this time based on automatically labeled words or phrases, is the one proposed in Turney (2002), which builds upon earlier work by Hatzivassiloglou and McKeown (1997). Starting with two reference words, *excellent* and *poor*, Turney classifies the polarity of a word or phrase by measuring the fraction between its pointwise mutual information (PMI) with the positive reference (excellent) and the PMI with the negative reference (poor). The PMI of two words w_1 and w_2 is defined as the probability of seeing the two words together divided by the probability of seeing each individual word: $PMI(w_1,w_2) = p(w_1,w_2)/ p(w_1)p(w_2)$. The polarity scores assigned in this way are used to automatically annotate the polarity of product, company, or movie reviews. Note that this system is completely unsupervised and thus particularly appealing for application to other languages.

Finally, when annotated corpora is available, machine-learning methods are a natural choice for building subjectivity and sentiment classifiers. For example (Wiebe et al., 1999) used a data set manually annotated for subjectivity to train a machine learning classifier, which led to significant improvements over the baseline. Similarly, starting with semiautomatically constructed data sets, Pang and Lee (2004) built classifiers for subjectivity annotation at sentence level, as well as a classifier for sentiment annotation at document level. To the extent that annotated data is available, such machine-learning classifiers can be used equally well in other languages.

Recently, a sentiment analysis tool based on deep learning techniques has been introduced in conjunction with a Sentiment Treebank (Socher et al., 2013), where fine-grained sentiment labels at word and phrase level are used together with a parse tree to compose the sentiment of a text. Unlike most of the earlier methods that assumed a text to have a consistent sentiment, this compositional method allows for changes of sentiment inside a text, as in "I generally like the phone, but I am not very fond of the tiny keyboard." Here, a positive and a negative sentiment are mixed in the same sentence.

Software and Data Sets for Sentiment Analysis

Sentiment analysis has received significant attention from both the research community and from commercial enterprises, with a sharp increase over the past 10 years in the amount of work devoted to this area. Many of the resources and tools described in this chapter are publicly available, even if in some cases their availability is restricted to research use only. Several sentiment and subjectivity lexicons are available, with various coverages, including OpinionFinder (http://mpqa.cs.pitt.edu/opinionfinder), General Inquirer (http://www.wjh.harvard.edu/~inquirer), and SentiWordNet (http://sentiwordnet.isti.cnr.it). Corpora publicly available, among others, are a movie review data set (http://www.cs.cornell.edu/people/pabo/movie-review-data), product review data sets (http://www.cs.uic.edu/~liub/FBS/sentiment-analysis.html#datasets), MPQA (http://mpqa.cs.pitt.edu/corpora/mpqa_corpus), and emotion and sentiment labeled data (http://web.eecs.umich.edu/~mihalcea/affectivetext). While tools for sentiment analysis can be easily built by applying off-the-shelf machine learning packages (such as Weka or Scikit, as described in Chapter 6) on sentiment analysis corpora, there are also more sophisticated tools such as deep learning implementations (http://nlp.stanford.edu/sentiment).

15

Topic Models

Learning Objectives

The goals of Chapter 15 are to help readers do the following:

1. Provide an overview of topic models and the theory of language on which they are based.

2. Review exemplary studies from multiple disciplines that use topic models to address theoretical and empirical research questions.

3. Review software packages and programming languages that are currently used by social scientists for topic modeling.

Topic modeling is a useful technique for researchers interested in identifying what topics are being discussed within a social group and how the topics being discussed shift over time as events unfold. This chapter provides an overview of the theory and practice of topic modeling, which has recently caught on with a wide range of researchers in the social sciences and humanities.

Topic modeling involves automated procedures for coding collections of texts in terms of meaningful categories that represent the main topics being discussed in the texts. Topic models assume that meanings are relational (Saussure, 1959) and that the meanings associated with a topic of conversation can be understood as a set of word clusters. Topic models treat texts as what linguists call a "bag of words," capturing word co-occurrences regardless of syntax, narrative, or location within a text. A topic can be thought of as the cluster of words that tend to come up in a discussion and therefore to co-occur more frequently than they otherwise would, whenever the topic is being discussed.

Topic modeling is generally more inductive than are most other approaches to text analysis (see Chapter 2). Instead of starting with predefined codes or categories derived from theory, researchers using topic models begin by specifying k, the number of topics they wish the algorithm to find. How to go about setting k is a highly technical issue discussed in numerous online forums and inter alia by Greene, O'Callahan, and Cunningham (2014). Selecting too few topics can produce results that are overly broad, while selecting too many leads to too many small, redundant topics. But once k is set, software (see the Software for Topic Modeling section in this chapter) identifies the specified number of topics, returns the probabilities of words being used in a topic, and provides an accounting of the distribution of those topics across the texts.

Topic modeling is an instance of probabilistic modeling, and the most widely used probabilistic model for topic modeling is latent Dirichlet allocation (LDA), which is a statistical model of language introduced by Blei, Ng, and Jordan (2003). LDA is based on the idea that every text within a texts collection is akin to a bag of words produced according to a mixture of topics that the author or authors intended to discuss. Each topic is a distribution over all observed words in the texts such that words that are strongly associated with the text's dominant topics have a higher chance of being included within the text's bag of words. Based on these distributions, authorship is conceptualized as an author repeatedly picking a topic and then a word and placing them in the bag until the document is complete. The objective of topic modeling is to find the parameters of the LDA process that has generated the final text or text collection, a process referred to as "inference" in the LDA literature. Among the outputs of the inference is a set of per-word topic distributions associating a probability with every topic–word pair and a similar set of per-topic text distributions describing the probability of choosing a particular topic for every specific text.

A second probabilistic model used in topic modeling is latent semantic analysis (LSA). LSA was first introduced as a distinct information retrieval technique for library indexing (Dumais, 2005). It is based on the similarity of meaning of words appearing in texts or passages (Foltz, Lauderr, & Laham, 1998) and presents words and texts using vector space modeling that compiles textual data into a term-by-document matrix, showing the weighted frequency of terms to represent the documents in the term space. LSA is based on singular value decomposition (SVD), which is closely associated with factor analysis, and represents terms and documents in a space of principal factors (Berry, Dumais, & O'Brien, 1995; Deerwester, Dumais, Furnas, Landauer, & Harshman, 1990). LSA employs a unique form of SVD, truncated SVD, which modifies term frequencies to include only terms of great importance in order to highlight underlying dimensions of the data. This process is very similar to principal component analysis, which is widely used in the social sciences.

In addition to LDA and LSA, computer scientists and statisticians have developed a number of other probabilistic models for identifying topics such as nonnegative matrix factorization (see Lee & Seung, 1999; Pauca, Shahnaz, Berry, & Plemmons, 2004). A different but related approach is employed in the text analysis software ALCESTE (Analyse des Lexèmes Co-occurents dans les Énnoncés Simples d'un Texte or analysis of the co-occurring lexemes within the simple statements of a text; also see the Software for Topic Modeling section at the end of this chapter). Originally developed by Max Reinert (1987), ALCESTE was designed to measure what Reinert termed *lexical worlds*, which he conceptualized as "mental rooms" that speakers successively inhabit, each with its own characteristic vocabulary. ALCESTE analyzes the distribution of words in a collection of texts based on the concepts of *statements*, *words*, and *similarity*. *Statements* are approximated natural sentences or natural fragments of sentences delimited by punctuation so as to have similar length. ALCESTE constructs a dictionary of lemmatized *words* referred to as "lexemes." To assess similarity between statements, ALCESTE constructs a matrix that crosses statements and words where the cells signal the presence or absence of a word (lexeme) within a statement. ALCESTE then performs a descending classification on this matrix, which produces classes of similar context units. The descending classification technique of ALCESTE maximizes the similarity between statements in the same class and also maximizes the difference between the classes. In the end, the user is provided with a series of classes and of statistical cues in the form of typical words, statements, authors, and so on, that provide a basis for interpreting the classes as lexical worlds, much as LSA and LDA interpret texts in terms of topics (see Brugidou et al., 2000). ALCESTE has been applied in sociology (Rousselière & Vézina, 2009; van Meter & Saint Léger, 2014), psychology (Lahlou, 1996; Noel-Jorand, Reinert, Bonnon, & Therme, 1995), political science (Bicquelet & Weale, 2011; Brugidou, 2003; Schonhardt-Bailey, 2013; Weale, Bicquelet, & Bara, 2012), management studies (Illia, Sonpar, & Bauer, 2014), and many other fields.

The use of topic models and ALCESTE within social science research projects brings with it a number of challenges. Social scientists need to be able to make sense of the topic word clusters that are produced by topic modeling software and to recognize when topics derived from algorithms are worthless or misleading. Ideally, topics will make sense to a subject area specialist or well-informed observer. Topic models require interpretive work, but topic models differ from other social science research methods in that in topic modeling, interpretive work occurs mainly *after* data is collected and analyzed. Topic models do the following:

[They] shift the locus of subjectivity within the methodological program—interpretation is still required, but from the perspective of the actual modeling of the data, the more subjective moment of the procedure has been shifted over to the post-modeling phase of the analysis. (Mohr & Bogdanov, 2013)

In using topic models, there is a significant risk of chimera topics (Schmidt, 2012), which are bogus topics that can occur because of various factors related to the data structure and interpretation. Most social scientists and humanities scholars are not yet using sophisticated diagnostics packages on their topic models (see Schmidt, 2012). And yet despite the challenges involved in modeling topics in large text collections and integrating topic models into theory-driven research designs, today topic models are being used by researchers in the humanities, political science, sociology, and other fields who often work collaboratively with computational linguists and other computer scientists.

Digital Humanities

Topic models have been embraced by many researchers in the humanities, and the field of digital humanities is dominated by topic modeling methods. The explosion of interest in topic models among humanists began in 2010 with widely circulated blog posts by Matthew L. Jockers on topic modeling and Cameron Blevins on a late 18th-century diary. Then, at an Institutes for Advanced Topics in the Digital Humanities conference in Los Angeles in 2010, several advocates of topic models, including David Mimno, David Blei, and David Smith, introduced the method to many humanities scholars for the first time. Since that conference, humanities scholars have used topic models in studies of themes in 19th-century literature (Jockers & Mimno, 2013), the history of literary scholarship (Goldstone & Underwood, 2012), and many other topics.

Political Science

Political scientists have used topic models to study a number of different categories of political phenomena. For instance, Quinn, Monroe, Colaresi, Crespin, and Radev (2010) analyzed topics in Senate floor speeches delivered between 1997 and 2004 using a database of over 118,000 speeches from the *Congressional Record*. Grimmer used topic models to develop the "expressed agenda model," which measures the attention senators allocate to press releases (Grimmer, 2010). His model simultaneously estimates the topics in the texts and the attention political actors allocate to the estimated topics. Gerrish and Blei (2012) have developed several predictive models linking legislative sentiment to legislative texts and have used these models to predict specific voting patterns with high levels of accuracy.

Sociology

Sociologists have used topic models mainly for analysis of historical data from newspaper and scholarly archives. For example, Paul DiMaggio, Manish Nag, and David Blei (2013) used LDA to investigate controversies that erupted over federal funding of the arts in the United States during the 1980s and 1990s. They coded almost 8,000 newspaper articles selected from five newspapers in order to analyze "frames," defined as sets of "discursive cues" that suggested a "particular interpretation of a person, event, organization, practice, condition, or situation" (DiMaggio, Nag, & Blei 2013, p. 593). DiMaggio and his colleagues found that different media frames were promoted by different institutional actors as a way to try to influence the course of public discourse and political debate. Of the 12 topics identified in their analysis, several clearly reflect politicized frames, such as the "1990s culture wars" and National Endowment for the Arts grant controversies.

Daniel McFarland and his colleagues have produced a series of studies employing various types of topic models as well as other text mining methodologies. In one study, they analyzed dissertation abstracts from 1980 to 2010, drawn from the ProQuest database of 240 U.S. research universities, to identify intellectual movements and trends. For example, looking only at the data from anthropology, their model was able to identify topics including archeology and a topic they labeled "identity studies."

Karen Levy and Michael Franklin (2013) used topic models to examine political contention in the U.S. trucking industry. Their data were online archives of public comments submitted during agency rulemakings, which they mined from the online portal regulations.gov. They used topic modeling to identify latent themes in a series of regulatory debates about electronic monitoring, finding that different types of commenters use different frames. Comments submitted by individuals were more likely to frame the electronic monitoring debate in terms of broader logistical problems plaguing the industry, such as long wait times at shippers' terminals. Organizational stakeholders were more likely to frame their comments in terms of technological standards and language relating to cost–benefit analysis.

Software for Topic Modeling

In the digital humanities and social sciences, the Java-based package MALLET (MAchine Learning for LanguagE Toolkit; http://mallet.cs.umass.edu) is widely used for topic modeling. MALLET performs statistical natural language processing, document classification, clustering, topic modeling, information extraction (IE), and other machine learning applications (see Chapters 5, 6, and 11 through 14). Because MALLET requires using the command line, it is most appropriate for users with at least moderate programming experience. But it typically uses only a small number of commands over and over so is relatively easy to learn (see http://mallet.cs.umass.edu/index.php). MALLET uses an implementation of Gibbs sampling, a statistical technique meant to quickly construct a sample distribution, to create its topic models. MALLET is also available as a package for R users, who can also use the packages topicmodels and LDA. Python offers the package Gensim (https://radimrehurek.com/gensim). Also note that a new package for humanities scholars, TOME (http://dhlab.lmc.gatech.edu/tome), is under development by a team at Georgia Tech.

As discussed in the beginning of this chapter, ALCESTE is a widely used alternative to topic modeling. The program is only available in a French language version in which all menus, commands, and outputs are in French, but it can be used on texts in English and other languages. It is available from the company Image (http://www.image-zafar.com/english/index_alceste.htm) and is not free, although an open source reproduction of ALCESTE is available in the Iramuteq interface for R (http://www.iramuteq.org).

Conclusions

PART V

16

Text Mining, Text Analysis, and the Future of Social Science

We have covered many topics in this book and in so doing have brought together ideas and techniques from the social sciences, humanities, and computer science. As we are not alone in seeking ways to integrate the social sciences more closely with computer science and related disciplines, in the remainder of this chapter we consider some of the different ways social scientists and computer scientists are working together to develop corpus-based and other types of digital research methods. While some social scientists have been working with computer scientists to develop digital versions of traditional research methods such as surveys, ethnographic interview techniques, and archival methods, others have been developing brand new research methods by engaging with computer science at a much deeper level. Such interdisciplinary engagement has resulted in the new fields of *computational social science* and *data science* and also in new forms of interdisciplinary research.

Computational social science is a relatively new field that can be dated to the second half of the 20th century and the invention of electronic computers. It is an "instrument-enabled scientific discipline" (Cioffi-Revilla, 2010), which is similar to microbiology, radio astronomy, or nanoscience in that it is a field in which the instrument of investigation (be it the microscope, radar, electron microscope, or microprocessor) drives the development of theory and empirical research. Contemporary computational social scientists use advanced computer hardware and software to analyze social phenomena that are "beyond the visible spectrum of traditional social science methods, or even beyond earlier statistical and mathematical approaches" (Cioffi-Revilla, 2010). The field is organized around five main types of computational methods: automated information extraction (IE), social network analysis, geospatial analysis, complexity modeling, and social simulation models. Each of these areas, in turn, has several specialized branches, and combinations among the five main methods are common (see Lazer et al., 2009).

A second field that has emerged at the intersection of social and computer science is data science. Where computational social science's home is mainly academia, data science is a new academic field that is closely tied to industry (O'Neil & Schutt, 2013). Data science involves handling large data sets (generated from social media, mobile phones, online purchases, genomes, and other sources) by integrating techniques and theories from many fields, including advanced computing, data warehousing, engineering, high-performance computing, math, pattern recognition and learning, statistics, visualization, and uncertainty modeling. Data science projects are usually handled by teams of specialists with varied backgrounds.

Although the very large data sets used in data science are likely to contain many errors, data scientists have found that massive but error-prone data sets can be more reliable than pristine but small samples. In a messy data set, "any particular reading may be incorrect, but the aggregate of many readings will provide a more comprehensive picture" (Mayer-Schönberger & Cukier, 2013, p. 34). Data science advocates often argue that big data entails a transition from research that searches for causation to research concerned only with correlation. Mayer-Schönberger and Cukier (2013) suggested the following:

> If millions of electronic medical records reveal that cancer sufferers who take a certain combination of aspirin and orange juice see their disease go into remission, then the exact cause for the improvement in health may be less important than the fact that they lived. Likewise, if we can save money by knowing the best time to buy a plane ticket without understanding the method behind airfare madness, that's good enough. (p. 14)

Although this shift away from trying to support or disprove theories may limit the possibility of biased sampling by the researcher, it can also lead to directionless inductive research (see Chapter 2) where the only answers that will be found are the ones the researcher has chosen to look for.

Social and Computer Science Collaboration

Computational social scientists and data scientists are both heavily involved in text mining and text analysis research. As we have seen in many chapters of this book, computational social science has made major contributions to the development of text mining and text analysis methods. However, in our view the composition of each field limits its potential contributions to social science research. The ability of computational social science to operate without making use of expert field knowledge limits the potential contributions of social and computer science collaboration. Hoffer, an anthropologist with extensive experience working with computational social scientists, makes this point when he suggests that results of computational social science simulations "rarely reflect the histories, concepts, relationships, interactions, and other nuances" (Hoffer, 2013, p. 19) that characterize social phenomena in the field. And while data science is an exciting new field, it is not a rapid discovery science but rather more like a form of engineering or applied science. There are "no innovations to be made in Data Science" because in the end the innovations to be in working with large data sets "are in Computer Science, Informatics, Statistics, Sociology, Visualization, Math, etc.—and they always will be" (McKelvey, 2013). Further, it appears in retrospect that the claims of at least some early prominent advocates of data science that the field would quickly do away with the scientific method (theory, hypotheses, attempts to establish causation) were naive at best and hark back to the inflated claims of social science history of the 1950s and 1960s (see Chapter 1). The consensus of members of the social science community who work with big data is that the scientific method is as valuable as ever and will continue to be used as long as researchers are interested not only in identifying patterns in data but in explaining the patterns they find (Pigliucci, 2009; Schradie, 2013).

Beyond interdisciplinary hybrids such as computational social science and data science, there are opportunities for collaboration and innovation at the intersection of social science and computer science because the two areas have something of a natural mutual affinity. Lee, Fielding, and Blank's (2008) discussion of the affinity between Google and the sociologist Robert Merton is instructive here. Lee, Fielding, and Blank (2008) noted that the one academic reference made by the founders of Google in their original patent was to one of Merton's studies of academic citation patterns. This suggests to us that the two fields are complementary at a deep and fundamental level: Whereas social scientists can gain from computer scientists' data mining and programming expertise, computer scientists need social scientists' expertise in research design, theory construction, case selection, sampling, and field knowledge (fine-grained in-depth knowledge of specific social, political, and cultural phenomena). One productive model for future development of text mining, text analysis, and other Internet-mediated research (IMR) methods is for social and computer scientists to learn some of their counterparts' methods and to develop bridging vocabulary for work on complex interdisciplinary research projects that require highly specialized research and technical skills (Hoffer, 2013, p. 22). Thus, we hope that in addition to providing practical guidance for using text mining methods for social research, this book can be seen as a viable model for further collaborative research between social and computer scientists.

• References •

Agirre, E., Cer, D., Diab, M., Gonzalez-Agirre, A., & Guo, W. (2013). SEM 2013 shared task: Semantic textual similarity. In *Second Joint Conference on Lexical and Computational Semantics (SEM), Volume 1: Proceedings of the Main Conference and the Shared Task* (pp. 32–43).

Alan Turing. (n.d.). In *Wikipedia*. Retrieved from https://en.wikipedia .org/wiki/Alan_Turing

Alm, C. O., Roth, D., & Sproat, R. (2005). Emotions from text: Machine learning for text-based emotion prediction. In *Proceedings of the Conference on Human Language Technology and Empirical Methods in Natural Language Processing* (pp. 579–586). Stroudsburg, PA: Association for Computational Linguistics.

Anderson, C. (2008, June 23). The end of theory: The data deluge makes the scientific method obsolete. *Wired*. Retrieved August 27, 2015, from http://archive.wired.com/science/ discoveries/magazine/16-07/pb_theory

Asher, K., & Ojeda, D. (2009). Producing nature and making the state: Ordenamiento Territorial in the Pacific Lowlands of Colombia. *Geoforum, 40*(3), 292–302.

Ayers, E. L. (1999). *The pasts and futures of digital history.* Retrieved June 17, 2015, from http://www.vcdh.virginia .edu/PastsFutures.html

Baker, P., Gabrielatos, C., Khosravinik, M., Krzyzanowski, M., Mcenery, T., & Wodak, R. (2008). A useful methodological synergy? Combining critical discourse analysis and corpus linguistics to examine discourses of refugees and asylum seekers in the UK press. *Discourse & Society, 19*(3), 273–306.

Balog, K., Mishne, G., & de Rijke, M. (2006). Why are they excited? Identifying and explaining spikes in blog mood levels. In *Proceedings of the Eleventh Meeting of the European Chapter of the Association for Computational Linguistics.* Stroudsburg, PA: Association for Computational Linguistics.

Bamberg, M. (2004). Talk, small stories, and adolescent identities. *Human Development, 47,* 366–369.

Banea, C., Mihalcea, R., Cardie, C., & Wiebe, J. (2014). The Spanish text similarity task. *Proceedings of the SemEval-2014 Workshop on Semantic Evaluation Exercises,* Dublin, Ireland.

Banfield, A. (1982). *Unspeakable sentences.* Boston, MA: Routledge and Kegan Paul.

Banko, M., Cafarella, M. J., Soderland, S., Broadhead, M., & Etzioni, O. (2007, January). Open information extraction from the web. *Communications of the ACM—Surviving the Data Deluge, 51*(12), 68–74.

Bauer, M. W., Bicquelet, A., & Suerdem, A. K. (2014). Text analysis: An introductory manifesto. In *Textual analysis (SAGE benchmarks in social research methods)* (Vol. 1). Thousand Oaks, CA: Sage.

Becker, H. S. (1993). How I learned what a crock was. *Journal of Contemporary Ethnography, 22,* 28–35.

Becker, L., & Denicolo, P. (2012). *Publishing journal articles (Success in research).* Thousand Oaks, CA: Sage.

Beer, F. A., & De Landtsheer, C. L. (2004). *Metaphorical world politics: Rhetorics of democracy, war and globalization.* East Lansing: Michigan State University Press.

Beer, F. A., & Harriman, R. (Eds.). (1996). *Post-realism: The rhetorical turn in international relations.* East Lansing: Michigan State University Press.

Bednarek, M., & Caple, H. (2014). Why do news values matter? Towards a new methodological framework for analyzing news discourse in critical discourse analysis and beyond. *Discourse & Society, 25*(2), 135–158.

Bell, E., Campbell, S., & Goldberg, L. R. (2015). Nursing identity and patient-centredness in scholarly health services research: A computational text analysis of PubMed Abstracts, 1986–2013. *BMC Health Services Research, 15*(3), 1–16.

Berelson, B. (1952). *Content analysis in communication research.* Glencoe, IL: Free Press.

Berglund, E. (2001). Facts, beliefs and biases: Perspectives on forest conservation in Finland. *Journal of Environmental Planning and Management, 44,* 833–849.

Berry, M. W., Dumais, S. T., & O'Brien, G. W. (1995). Using linear algebra for intelligent information retrieval. *SIAM Review, 37*(4), 573–595.

Bicquelet, A., & Weale, A. (2011). Coping with the cornucopia: Can text mining help handle the data deluge in public policy analysis? *Policy and Internet*, *3*(4), 1–21.

Biernacki, R. (2014). Humanist interpretation versus coding text samples. *Qualitative Sociology*, *37*(2), 173–188.

Birke, J., & Sarkar, A. (2007). Active learning for the identification of nonliteral language. In *Proceedings of the Workshop on Computational Approaches to Figurative Language* (pp. 21–28). Stroudsburg, PA: Association for Computational Linguistics.

Birnbaum, M. H. (2000). Decision making in the lab and on the web. In M. H. Birnbaum (Ed.), *Psychological experiments on the Internet* (pp. 3–34). San Diego, CA: Academic Press.

Blei, D. M., Ng, A. Y., & Jordan, M. I. (2003). Latent dirichlet allocation. *Journal of Machine Learning Research*, *3*, 993–1022.

Boroditsky, L. (2000). Metaphoric structuring: Understanding time through spatial metaphors. *Cognition*, *75*(1), 1–28.

Boyatzis, R. E. (1998). *Transforming qualitative information: Thematic analysis and code development*. Thousand Oaks, CA: Sage.

Bradley, J. (1989). *TACT, Version 1, User's guide*. Toronto, Canada: University of Toronto Computing Services.

Braun, V., & Clarke, V. (2006). Using thematic analysis in psychology. *Qualitative Research in Psychology*, *3*(2), 77–101.

Brin, S., Davis, J., & Garca-Molina, H. (1995). Copy detection mechanisms for digital documents. *ACM International Conference on Management of Data*, *24*(2), 398–409.

Broder, A. Z., Ciccolo, P., Fontoura, M., Gabrilovich, E., Josifovsk, V., & Riedel, L. (2008). Search advertising using web relevance feedback. In *CIKM '08: Proceeding of the Seventeenth ACM Conference on Information and Knowledge Management* (pp. 1013–1022). New York, NY: Association for Computing Machinery.

Broder, A. Z., Glassman, S. C., Manasse, M. S., & Zweig, G. (1997). Syntactic clustering of the web. *Computer Networks and ISDN Systems*, *29*(8–13), 1157–1166.

Brugidou, M. (2003). Argumentation and values: An analysis of ordinary political competence via an open-ended question. *International Journal of Public Opinion Research*, *15*(4), 413–430.

Brugidou M., Escoffier, C., Folch, H., Lahlou, S., Le Roux, D., Morin-Andreani, P., & Piat, G. (2000). Les facteurs de choix et d'utilisation de logiciels d'Analyse de Données Textuelles. In *JADT 2000 (5èmes Journées Internationales d'Analyse Statistique des Données Textuelles)*.

Bruner, J. S. (1990). *Acts of meaning*. Cambridge, MA: Harvard University Press.

Buchholz, M. B., & von Kleist, C. (1995). *Psychotherapeutische Interaktion: Qualitative studien zu konversation und metapher, geste und plan*. Opladen, Germany: Westdeutscher Verlag.

Budanitsky, A., & Hirst, G. (2001). Semantic distance in WordNet: An experimental, application-oriented evaluation of five measures. In *Proceedings of the NAACL Workshop on WordNet and Other Lexical Resources*, *2*, 8–13

Budge, I. (2001). "Theory and Measurement of Party Policy Positions." In I. Budge, H.-D. Klingemann, A. Volkens, J. Bara, & E. Tanenbaum (eds.), *Mapping Policy Preferences: Estimates for Parties, Electors, and Governments 1945–1998*. Oxford: Oxford University Press.

Cameron, L. (2003). *Metaphor in educational discourse*. New York, NY: Continuum.

Carenini, G., Ng, R., & Zhou, X. (2007). Summarizing emails with conversational cohesion and subjectivity. In *Proceedings of the Sixteenth International Conference on World Wide Web*. New York, NY: Association for Computing Machinery.

Carlson, A., Betteridge, J., Kisiel, B., Settles, B., Hruschka, E. R., Jr., & Mitchell, T. M. (2010, July). Toward an architecture for never-ending language learning. In *Proceedings of the Twenty-Fourth American Association for Artificial Intelligence Conference on Artificial Intelligence* (pp. 1306–1313). Cambridge, MA: AAAI Press.

Carver, T., & Pikalo, J. (2008). *Political language and metaphor: Interpreting and changing the world*. New York, NY: Routledge.

Cerulo, K. A. (1998). *Deciphering violence: The cognitive structure of right and wrong*. New York, NY: Routledge.

Charteris-Black, J. (2009). Metaphor and political communication. In A. Musolff & J. Zinken (Eds.), *Metaphor and discourse* (pp. 97–115). Basingstoke, Hampshire, England: Palgrave Macmillan.

Charteris-Black, J. (2012). Comparative keyword analysis and leadership communication: Tony Blair—A study of rhetorical style. In L. Helms (Ed.), *Comparative political leadership* (pp. 142–164). Basingstoke, England: Palgrave Macmillan.

Charteris-Black, J. (2013). *Analysing political speeches: Rhetoric, discourse and metaphor.* Basingstoke, England: Palgrave Macmillan.

Chilton, P. (1996). *Security metaphors: Cold War discourse from containment to common house.* New York, NY: Peter Lang.

Church, K. W., & Hanks, P. (1990). Word association norms, mutual information, and lexicography. *Computational Linguistics, 16*(1), 22–29.

Cioffi-Revilla, C. (2010). Computational social science. *WILEY Interdisciplinary Reviews: Computational Statistics, 2*(3), 259–271.

Coffey, A., Holbrook, B., & Atkinson, P. (1996). Qualitative data analysis: Technologies and representations. *Sociological Research Online, 1*(1), 44.

Cohen, D. J., & Rosenzweig, R. (2005). *Digital history: A guide to gathering, preserving, and presenting the past on the web.* Philadelphia: University of Pennsylvania Press.

Colley, S. K., & Neal, A. (2012). Automated text analysis to examine qualitative differences in safety schema among upper managers, supervisors and workers. *Safety Science, 50*(9), 1775–1785.

Collins, C., Viégas, F. B., & Wattenberg, M. (2009). Parallel tag clouds to explore and analyze faceted text corpora. *IEEE Symposium on Visual Analytics Science and Technology.* Retrieved from ieeexplore.ieee.org/xpls/abs_all.jsp?arnumber=5333443&tag=1

Collins, M. (2003). Head-driven statistical models for natural language

parsing. *Computational Linguistics, 29*(4), 589–637.

Couper, M. P. (2000). Web surveys: A review of issues and approaches. *Public Opinion Quarterly, 64*(4), 464–494.

Creswell, J. D. (2014). *Research design: Qualitative, quantitative, and mixed methods approaches.* Thousand Oaks, CA: Sage.

Cunningham, G. B., Sagas, M., Sartore, M. L., Amsden, M. L., & Schellhase, A. (2004). Gender representation in the *NCAA News*: Is the glass half full or half empty? *Sex Roles, 50*(11–12), 861–870.

Dagan, I., Glickman, O., & Magnini, B. (2006). The PASCAL recognising textual entailment challenge. In *Proceedings of the PASCAL Workshop, 3944,* 177–190.

Danescu-Niculescu-Mizil, C., Lee, L., Pang, B., & Kleinberg, J. (2012). Echoes of power: Language effects and power differences in social interaction. *WWW.* Retrieved August 27, 2015, from https://5harad.com/mse331/papers/danescu_et_al_power.pdf

De Landtsheer, C., & De Vrij, I. (2004). Talking about Srebrenica: Dutch elites and Dutchbat. How metaphors change during crisis. In F. A. Beer & C. De Landtsheer (Eds.), *Metaphorical world politics. Rhetorics of democracy, war and globalization* (pp. 163–189). East Lansing: Michigan State University Press.

Deerwester, S., Dumais, S., Furnas, G., Landauer, T., & Harshman, R. (1990). Indexing by latent semantic analysis. *Journal of the American Society for Information Science, 41*(6), 391–407.

Denzin, N. K, & Lincoln, Y. S. (2011). Epilogue: Toward a "refunctioned ethnography." *The SAGE Handbook of Qualitative Research.* Thousand Oaks, CA: Sage.

DiMaggio, P., Nag, M., & Blei, D. (2013). Exploiting affinities between topic modeling and the sociological perspective on culture: Application to newspaper coverage of U.S. government arts funding. *Science Direct, 41*(6), 570–606.

Dohan, D., Abramson, C. M., & Miller, S. (2012). Beyond text: Using arrays of ethnographic data to identify causes and construct narratives. Paper presented at the American Journal of Sociology Conference on Causal Thinking and Ethnographic Research, Chicago, IL.

Dolan, W., Quirk, C., & Brockett, C. (2004). Unsupervised construction of large paraphrase corpora: Exploiting massively parallel news sources. *COLING '04 Proceedings of the Twentieth International Conference on Computational Linguistics, 350.* Stroudsburg, PA: Association for Computational Linguistics.

Dumais, S. T. (2005). Latent semantic analysis. *Annual Review of Information Science and Technology, 38*(1), 188–230.

Durland, M. M., & Fredericks, K. A. (2005). Social network analysis in program evaluation. *New Directions in Evaluation, 107.*

Edley, N., & Wetherell, M. (1997). Jockeying for position: The construction of masculine identities. *Discourse & Society, 8*(2), 203–217.

Egozi, O., Markovitch, S., & Gabrilovich, E. (2011). Concept-based information retrieval using explicit semantic analysis. *ACM Transactions on Information Systems, 29*(2), 8.

Esuli, A., & Sebastiani, F. (2006a). Determining term subjectivity and term orientation for opinion mining. In *Proceedings of the Eleventh Conference of the European Chapter of the Association for*

Computational Linguistics, Trento, Italy. Abstract retrieved from http://citeseerx.ist.psu.edu/viewdoc/summary?doi=10.1.1.60.8645

Esuli, A., & Sebastiani, F. (2006b). SentiWordNet: A publicly available lexical resource for opinion mining. In *Proceedings of the Fifth Conference on Language Resources and Evaluation*, Genova, Italy. Abstract retrieved from http://citeseerx.ist.psu.edu/viewdoc/summary?doi=10.1.1.61.7217

Etzioni, O., Cafarella, M., Downey, D., Kok, S., Popescu, A. M., Shaked, T., . . . Yates, A. (2004). Web-scale information extraction in knowitall:(preliminary results). In *Proceedings of the Thirteenth International Conference on World Wide Web* (pp. 100–110). New York, NY: Association for Computing Machinery.

Evison, J. (2013). Turn openings in academic talk: Where goals and roles intersect. *Classroom Discourse, 4*(1), 3–26.

Fairclough, N. (1992). Intertextuality in critical discourse analysis. *Science Direct, 4*(3–4), 269–293.

Fairclough, N. (1995). *Critical discourse analysis: The critical study of language*. London, England: Longman.

Fader, A., Soderland, S., & Etzioni, O. (2011). Identifying relations for open information extraction. In *Proceedings of the Conference on Empirical Methods in Natural Language Processing* (pp. 1535–1545). Stroudsburg, PA: Association for Computational Linguistics.

Fass, D. (1991). Met*: A method for discriminating metonymy and metaphor by computer. *Computer Linguistics, 17*(1), 49–90.

Fellbaum, C. (Ed.). (1998). *WordNet: An electronic lexical database*. Cambridge, MA: MIT Press.

Fenton, F. (1911). The influence of newspaper presentations upon the growth of crime and other anti-social activity. *American Journal of Sociology, 16*(3), 342–371.

Fernandez, J. W. (1991). *Beyond metaphor: The theory of tropes in anthropology*. Stanford, CA: Stanford University Press.

Finkelstein, L., Gabrilovich, E., Matias, Y., Rivlin, E., Solan, Z., Wolfman, G., & Ruppin, E. (2001). Placing search in context: The concept revisited. In *Proceedings of the Tenth International Conference on World Wide Web* (pp. 406–414). Stroudsburg, PA: Association for Computational Linguistics.

Flyvbjerg, B. (2001). *Making social science matter: Why social inquiry fails and how it can succeed again*. Cambridge, England: The Press Syndicate of the University of Cambridge.

Foltz, P. W., Lauderr, T. K., & Laham, D. (1998). An introduction to latent semantic analysis. *Discourse Processes, 25*(2–3), 259–284.

Foucault, M. (1973). *The order of things: An archaeology of the human sciences*. New York, NY: Vintage Books.

Foucault, M. (1975). *The birth of the clinic: An archaeology of medical perception*. New York, NY: Vintage Books.

Franklin, S. (2002). Bialowieza Forest, Poland: Representation, myth, and the politics of dispossession. *Environment and Planning, 34*, 1459–1485.

Franzosi, R. (2010). *Quantitative narrative analysis*. Thousand Oaks, CA: Sage.

Franzosi, R. (2012). The difficulty of mixed-method approaches. *Sociological Methodology, 42*(1), 79–81.

Franzosi, R., De Fazio, G., & Vicari, S. (2012). Ways of measuring agency: An application of quantitative narrative analysis to lynchings in Georgia (1875–1930). *Sociological Methodology, 42*(1), 1–42.

Franzosi, R., Doyle, S., McClelland, L. E., Putnam Rankin, C., & Vicari, S. (2013). Quantitative narrative analysis software options compared: PC-ACE and CAQDAS (ATLAS.ti, MAXqda, and NVivo). *Quality & Quantity, 47*(6), 3219–3247.

Freud, S. (2011). *From the history of an infantile neurosis—A classic article on psychoanalysis*. Redditch, Worcestershire, England: Read Books. (Original work published 1918)

Frith, H., & Gleeson, K. (2004). Clothing and embodiment: Men managing body image and appearance. *Psychology of Men & Masculinity, 5*(1), 40–48.

Fung, K. (2013). *Numbersense: How to use big data to your advantage*. New York, NY: McGraw-Hill Education.

Gabrilovich, E., & Shaul M. (2007). Computing semantic relatedness using Wikipedia-based explicit semantic analysis. In R. Sangal, H. Mehta, & R. K. Bagga (Eds.), *Proceedings of the International Joint Conference on Artificial Intelligence* (pp. 1606–1611). San Francisco, CA: Morgan Kaufmann Publishers.

Gandy, L., Nadji, A., Atallah, M., Frieder, O., Howard, N., Kanareykin, S., . . . Argamon, S. (2013). Automatic identification of conceptual metaphors with limited knowledge. In *Proceedings of the Twenty-Seventh AAAI Conference on Artificial Intelligence*. Cambridge, MA: AAAI Press.

Garton, L., Haythornthwaite, C., & Wellman, B. (1997). Studying online social networks. *Journal of Computer Mediated Communication, 3*(1).

Gee, J. P. (1991). A linguistic approach to narrative. *Journal of Narrative and Life History, 1*(1), 15–39.

Gerrish, S., & Blei, D. (2012). How they vote: Issue-adjusted models of legislative behavior. *Neural Information Processing Systems.* Retrieved June 26, 2015, from https://www.cs.princeton.edu/~blei/papers/GerrishBlei2012.pdf

Gibbs, R. W. (1994). *The poetics of mind: Figurative thought, language, and understanding.* Cambridge, England: Cambridge University Press.

Gibson, C. B., & Zellmer-Bruhn, M. E. (2001). Metaphors and meaning: An intercultural analysis of the concept of teamwork. *Administrative Science Quarterly, 46*(2), 274–303.

Glaser, B., & Strauss, A. L. (1967). *The discovery of grounded theory: Strategies for qualitative research.* Piscataway, NJ: Transaction Publishers.

Goatly, A. (2007). *Washing the brain: Metaphor and hidden ideology.* Philadelphia, PA: John Benjamins Publishing Company.

Goble, E., Austin, W., Larsen, D., Kreitzer, L., & Brintnell, E. S. (2012). Habits of mind and the split-mind effect: When computer-assisted qualitative data analysis software is used in phenomenological research. *Forum: Qualitative Social Research, 13*(2). Retrieved from http://www.qualitative-research.net/index.php/fqs/article/view/1709

Golden, S. (2010). Sociologists might be Yahoo's competitive advantage. *The Society Pages.* Retrieved June 27, 2015, from thesocietypages.org/clippings/2010/01/12/sociologists-might-be-yahoos-competitive-advantage

Goldstone, A., & Underwood, T. (2012). What can topic models of

PMLA teach us about the history of literary scholarship? *The stone and the shell.* Retrieved June 27, 2015, from tedunderwood.com/2012/12/14/what-can-topic-models-of-pmla-teach-us-about-the-history-of-literary-scholarship

Golub, G. H., & Reinsch, C. (1970). Singular value decomposition and least squares solutions. *Numerische Mathematic, 14,* 403–420.

González-Ibáñez, R., Muresan, S., & Wacholder, N. (2011). Identifying sarcasm in Twitter: A closer look. In *Proceedings of the Forty-Ninth Annual Meeting of the Association for Computational Linguistics: Human Language Technologies*—Short Papers Volume 2. Stroudsburg, PA: Association for Computational Linguistics.

Goodrum, A. (2000). Image information retrieval: An overview of current research. *Informing Science, 3*(2), 63–66.

Gorard, S. (2013). *Research design: Creating robust approaches for the social sciences.* Thousand Oaks, CA: Sage

Greene, D., O'Callahan, D., & Cunningham, P. (2014). How many topics? Stability analysis for topic models. In T. Calders, F. Esposito, E. Hüllermeier, & R. Meo (Eds.), Lecture Notes in Computer Science: Vol. 8724. Machine Learning and Knowledge Discovery in Databases (pp. 498–513). doi:10.1007/978-3-662-44848-9_32

Gregory, M. L., Chinchor, N. A., Whitney, P., Carter, R., Hetzler, E., & Turner, A. (2006). User-directed sentiment analysis: Visualizing the affective content of documents. *Proceedings of the Workshop on Sentiment and Subjectivity in Text, Sydney, Australia* (pp. 23–30). Stroudsburg, PA: Association for Computational Linguistics.

Grimmer, J. (2010). A Bayesian hierarchical topic model for political texts: Measuring expressed agendas in Senate press releases. *Oxford Journals, 18*(1), 1–35

Grimmer, J., & Stewart, B. M. (2013). Text as data: The promise and pitfalls of automatic content analysis methods for political texts. *Political Analysis, 21*(3), 267–297.

Hakimnia, R., Holmström, I. K., Carlsson, M., & Höglund, A. T. (2014). Exploring the communication between telenurse and caller—A critical discourse analysis. *International Journal of Qualitative Studies on Health and Well-Being, 9.*

Halliday, M. A. K. (2006). Systemic background. In J. J. Webster (Ed.), *On language and linguistics: Volume 3 in the collected works of M. A. K. Halliday* (p. 186). New York, NY: Bloomsbury Academic. (Reprinted from *Systemic perspectives on discourse, Vol. 1: Selected theoretical papers. The Ninth International Systemic Workshop,* by J. D. Benson & W. S. Greaves, Eds., 1985, New York, NY: Ablex)

Hansford, T. G., & Coe, C. (2014). *Linguistic complexity and public acceptance of Supreme Court decisions.* Retrieved from August 27, 2015, http://faculty.ucmerced.edu/thansford/Working%20Papers/Hansford_Coe_Complexity_APSA.pdf

Hardie, A., Koller, V., Rayson, P., & Semino, E. (2007). Exploiting a semantic annotation tool for metaphor analysis. In M. Davies, P. Rayson, S. Hunston, & P. Danielsson (Eds.), *Proceedings of the Corpus Linguistics 2007 Conference.* Retrieved from ucrel.lancs.ac.uk/people/paul/publications/HardieEtAl_CL2007.pdf

Harris, J. (2011). Word clouds considered harmful. *Nieman Journalism Lab.* Retrieved from http://

www.niemanlab.org/2011/10/word-clouds-considered-harmful

Hart, C. (2010). *Critical discourse analysis and cognitive science: New perspectives on immigration discourse.* Basingstoke, England: Palgrave Macmillan.

Hassan, S., & Mihalcea, R. (2009). Cross-lingual semantic relatedness using encyclopedic knowledge. *Proceedings of the Conference on Empirical Methods in Natural Language Processing* (pp. 1192–1201). Stroudsburg, PA: Association for Computational Linguistics.

Hassan, S., & Mihalcea, R. (2011). Semantic relatedness using salient semantic analysis. *Proceedings of the Conference of the American Association for Artificial Intelligence* Cambridge, MA: AAAI Press.

Hatzivassiloglou, V., & McKeown, K. (1997). Predicting the semantic orientation of adjectives. In *Proceedings of the Thirty-Fifth Annual Meeting of the Association for Computational Linguistics and Eighth Conference of the European Chapter of the Association for Computational Linguistics* (pp. 174–181). Stroudsburg, PA: Association for Computational Linguistics.

Heath, C., & Luff, P. (2000). *Technology in action.* Cambridge, England: Cambridge University Press.

Heintze, N. (1996). Scalable document fingerprinting. *In Proc. USENIX Workshop on Electronic Commerce.* Murray Hill, NJ: Bell Laboratories.

Henderson, S., & Segal, E. H. (2013). Visualizing qualitative data in evaluation research. *New Directions for Evaluation, 139,* 53–71.

Heritage, J., & Raymond, G. (2005). The terms of agreement: Indexing epistemic authority and subordination

in talk-in-interaction. *Social Psychology Quarterly, 68*(1), 15–38.

Hewson, C., & Laurent, D. (2012). Research design and tools for Internet research. In J. Hughes (Ed.), *Sage Internet research methods: Volume 1.* Thousand Oaks, CA: Sage.

Hewson, C., Yule, P., Laurent, D., & Vogel, C. (Eds.). (2003). *Internet research methods: A practical guide for the social and behavioural sciences.* Thousand Oaks, CA: Sage.

Hine, C. (2000). *Virtual ethnography.* Thousand Oaks, CA: Sage.

Hine, C. (2005). *Virtual methods.* Oxford, England: Berg.

Hirschman, E. C. (1987). People as products: Analysis of a complex marketing exchange. *Journal of Marketing, 51*(1), 98–108.

Hoad, T. C., & Zobel, J. (2003). Methods for identifying versioned and plagiarized documents. *Journal of American Society Information Science Technology, 54*(3), 203–215.

Hoffer, L.D. (2013). Unreal models of real behavior: The agent-based modeling experience. *Practicing Anthropology, 35*(1), 19–23.

Hofstede, G. (1980). *Culture's consequences: International differences in work-related values.* Beverly Hills, CA: Sage.

Holland, D., & Quinn, N. (1987). *Cultural models in language and thought.* New York, NY: Press Syndicate of the University of Cambridge.

Howell, D. C. (2013). *Fundamental statistics for the behavioral sciences.* Belmont, CA: Wadsworth Cengage Learning.

Hu, M., & Liu, B. (2004). Mining and summarizing customer reviews. In

Proceedings of the Tenth ACM SIGKDD International Conference on Knowledge Discovery and Data Mining (pp. 168–177). New York, NY: Association for Computing Machinery.

Ignatow, G. (2003). "Idea hamsters" on the "bleeding edge": Profane metaphors in high technology jargon. *Poetics, 31*(1), 1–22.

Ignatow, G. (2004). Speaking together, thinking together? Exploring metaphor and cognition in a shipyard union dispute." *Sociological Forum, 19*(3), 405–433.

Ignatow, G. (2009). Culture and embodied cognition: Moral discourses in Internet support groups for overeaters. *Social Forces, 88*(2), 643–669.

Ignatow, G. (2015, February 27). Theoretical foundations for digital text analysis. *Journal for the Theory of Social Behaviour.* Advance online publication. doi:10.1111/jtsb.12086

Ilieva, J., Baron, S., & Healey, N. M. (2002). Online surveys in marketing research: Pros and cons. *International Journal of Market Research, 44*(3), 361–376.

Illia, L., Sonpar, K., & Bauer, M. W. (2014). Applying co-occurrence text analysis with ALCESTE to studies of impression management. *British Journal of Management, 25*(2), 352–372.

Illouz, E. (2008). *Saving the modern soul: Therapy, emotions, and the culture of self-help.* Berkeley: University of California Press.

Islam, A., & Inkpen, D. (2008). Semantic text similarity using corpus-based word similarity and string similarity. *ACM Transactions on Knowledge Discovery From Data, 2*(2), 1–25.

Islam, A., & Inkpen, D. (2009). Semantic similarity of short texts.

Recent Advances in Natural Language Processing V: Vol. 309. Current Issues in Linguistic Theory (pp. 227–236). Amsterdam, The Netherlands: John Benjamins.

Jiang, J. J., & Conrath, D. W. (1997). Semantic similarity based on corpus statistics and lexical taxonomy. *Proceedings of the International Conference on Research in Computational Linguistics*, Taiwan.

Jockers, M. L., & Mimno, D. (2013). Significant themes in 19th-century literature. *Poetics, 41*(6), 750–769.

Johnson-Laird, P. N. (1983). *Mental models: Toward a cognitive science of language, inference, and consciousness.* Cambridge, England: Cambridge University Press.

Johnson-Laird, P. N. (1989). *Mental models.* Cambridge, MA: MIT Press.

Jones, M. V., Coviello, Y., & Tang, Y. K. (2011). International entrepreneurship research (1989–2009): A domain ontology and thematic analysis. *Journal of Business Venturing, 26*(6), 632–649.

Kalo, Z., & Racz, J. (2014). *Systematic conceptual metaphor analysis with ATLAS.ti.* Paper presented at the CAQDAS 2014 Conference, University of Surrey, Australia. Retrieved from https://www.surrey.ac.uk/sociology/ research/researchcentres/caqdas/ files/Kalo+Racz_CAQ14_Systematic_ Conceptual_Metaphor_Analysis_with_ ATLASti.pdf

Kempton, W. (1987). Two theories of home heat control. *Cognitive Science, 10*(1), 75–90.

Kim, S.-M., & Hovy, E. (2006). Identifying and analyzing judgment opinions. In *Proceedings of the Main Conference on Human Language Technology Conference of the North American Chapter of the Association of*

Computational Linguistics. Stroudsburg, PA: Assocation for Computational Linguistics.

King, A. (2008). In vivo coding. In L. Given (Ed.), *The SAGE encyclopedia of qualitative research methods.* Thousand Oaks, CA: Sage.

Klein, D., & Manning, C. D. (2004). Corpus-based induction of syntactic structure: Models of dependency and constituency. In *Proceedings of the Forty-Second Annual Meeting of the Association for Computational Linguistics.* Stroudsburg, PA: Association for Computational Linguistics.

Koller, V., & Mautner, G. (2004). Computer applications in critical discourse analysis. In *Applying English Grammar* (pp. 216–228). London, England: Hodder and Stoughton.

Koppel, M., Argamon, S., & Shimoni, A. R. (2002). Automatically categorizing written texts by author gender. *Literary and Linguistic Computing, 17*(4), 401–412.

Kovecses, Z. (2002). *Metaphor: A practical introduction.* Oxford, England: Oxford University Press.

Kozinets, R. V. (2002). The field behind the screen: Using netnography for marketing research in online communities. *Journal of Marketing Research, 39*(1), 61–72.

Kozinets, R. V. (2009). *Netnography: Doing ethnographic research online.* Thousand Oaks, CA: Sage.

Krippendorff, K. H. (2013). *Content analysis: An introduction to its methodology.* Thousand Oaks, CA: Sage.

Krishnamurthy, R. (1996). Ethnic, racial and tribal: The language of racism? In C. R. Caldas-Coulthard & M. Coulthard (Eds.), *Texts and practices: Readings in critical discourse analysis* (pp. 129–149). London, England: Routledge.

Krueger, R. A., & Casey, M. A. (2014). *Focus groups: A practical guide for applied research.* Thousand Oaks, CA: Sage.

Labov, W. (1972). *Sociolinguistic patterns.* Philadelphia: University of Pennsylvania Press.

Labov, W., & Waletzky, J. (1967). Narrative analysis. In J. Helm (Ed.), *Essays on the verbal and visual arts* (pp. 12–44). Seattle: University of Washington Press.

Lahlou, S. (1996). A method to extract social representations from linguistic corpora. *Japanese Journal of Experimental Social Psychology, 35*(3), 278–291.

Lakoff, G. (1987). *Women, fire, and dangerous things. What categories reveal about the mind.* Chicago, IL: University of Chicago Press.

Lakoff, G. (1996). *Moral politics: How liberals and conservatives think.* Chicago, IL: University of Chicago Press.

Lakoff, G., & Johnson, M. (1980). *Metaphors we live by.* Chicago, IL: University of Chicago Press.

Lakoff, G., & Johnson, M. (1999). *Philosophy in the flesh.* New York, NY: Basic Books.

Landauer, T. K., Foltz, P. W., & Laham, D. (1998). An introduction to latent semantic analysis. *Discourse Processes, 25*(2–3), 259–284.

Lasswell, H. (1927). Propaganda technique in the world war. *American Political Science Review, 21*(3), 627–631.

Lazer, D., Kennedy, R., King, G., & Vespignani, A. (2014). The parable of Google flu: Traps in big data analysis. *Science, 343*(6176), 1203–1205. Retrieved August 27, 2015, from http://gking.harvard.edu/files/gking/files/0314policyforumff.pdf

Lazer, D., Pentland, A., Adamic, L., Aral, S., Barabási, A.-L., Brewer, D., . . . Van Alstyne, M. (2009). Computational social science. *Science, 323*(5915), 721–723.

Leacock, C., & Chodorow, M. (1998). Combining local context and WordNet sense similarity for word sense identification. In *WordNet, an electronic lexical database* (pp. 265–283). Cambridge, MA: MIT Press.

Leacock, C., Chodorow, M., & Miller, G. A. (1998). Using corpus statistics and WordNet relations for sense identification. *Computational Linguistics, 24*(1), 147–165.

Lee, B., Riche, N. H., Karlson, A. K., & Carpendale, S. (2010). SparkClouds: Visualizing trends in tag clouds. *Visualization and Computer Graphics, IEEE Transactions on Knowledge and Data Engineering, 16*(6), 1182–1189.

Lee, D. D., & Seung, S. (1999). Learning the parts of objects by non-negative matrix factorization. *Nature, 401,* 788–791.

Lee, M. D., Pincombe, B., & Welsh, M. (2005). *An empirical evaluation of models of text document similarity* (pp. 1254–1259). Mahwah, NJ: Lawrence Erlbaum.

Lee, R. M., Fielding, N. G., & Blank, G. (2008). The Internet as a research medium. In N. G. Fielding, R. M. Lee, & G. Blank (Eds.), *The SAGE handbook of online research methods* (pp. 3–20). Thousand Oaks, CA: Sage.

Leong, C. W., & Mihalcea, R. (2009). Explorations in automatic image annotation using textual features. *Proceedings of the Third Linguistic Annotation Workshop* (pp. 56–59). Stroudsburg, PA: Association for Computational Linguistics.

LeRoux, B., & Rouanet, H. (2010). *Multiple correspondence analysis.* Thousand Oaks, CA: Sage.

Lesk, M. (1986). Automatic sense disambiguation using machine readable dictionaries: How to tell a pine cone from an ice cream cone. *Proceedings of the SIGDOC Conference 1986* (pp. 24–26). New York, NY: Association for Computing Machinery.

Levy, K. E. C., & Franklin, M. (2014). Driving regulation: Using topic models to examine political contention in the United States trucking industry. *Social Science Computer Review, 32*(2), 182–194.

Li, Y., McLean, D., Bandar, Z. A., O'Shea, J. D., & Crockett, K. (2006). Sentence similarity based on semantic nets and corpus statistics. *IEEE Transactions on Knowledge and Data Engineering, 18*(8), 1138–1150.

Lin, C.-Y., & Hovy, E. (2003). Automatic evaluation of summaries using N-gram co-occurrence statistics. *Proceedings of Human Language Technology Conference (HLT- NAACL [2003])* (pp. 71–78). Stroudsburg, PA: Association for Computational Linguistics.

Lin, D. (1998). An information-theoretic definition of similarity. *Proceedings of the Fifteenth International Conference on Machine Learning* (pp. 296–304). San Francisco, CA: Morgan Kaufmann Publishers.

Lipton, P. (2003). *Inference to the best explanation.* New York, NY: Routledge.

List of Wikipedias. (n.d.). In *Wikipedia.* Retrieved from https://meta.wikimedia.org/wiki/List_of_Wikipedias

Liu, B., & Mihalcea, R. (2007). Of men, women, and computers: Data-driven gender modeling for improved user interfaces. Paper presented at the Proceedings of the International Conference on Weblogs and Social Media, Boulder, CO.

Lloyd, L., Kechagias, D., & Skiena, S. (2005). Lydia: A system for large-scale news analysis. *String Processing and Information Retrieval, 3372,* 161–166.

London School of Economics. (2012). Five minutes with Prabhakar Raghavan: Big data and social science at Google. Retrieved May 28, 2015, from http://blogs.lse.ac.uk/impactofsocialsciences/2012/09/19/five-minutes-with-prabhakar-raghavan

Maas, A. L., Daly, R. E., Pham, P. T., Huang, D., Ng, A. Y., & Potts, C. (2011). Learning word vectors for sentiment analysis. In *Proceedings of the Forty-Ninth Annual Meeting of the Association for Computational Linguistics: Human Language Technologies.* Stroudsburg, PA: Association for Computational Linguistics.

Macmillan, K. (2005). More than just coding? Evaluating CAQDAS in a discourse analysis of news texts. *Forum: Qualitative Social Research, 6*(3). Retrieved from qualitative-research.net/index.php/fqs/article/view/28

Macy, M. W., & Willer, R. (2002). From factors to actors: Computational sociology and agent-based modeling. *Annual Review of Sociology, 28*(1), 143–166.

Mairesse, F., Walker, M., Mehl, M., & Moore, R. (2007). Using linguistic cues for the automatic recognition of personality in conversation and text. *Journal of Artificial Intelligence Research, 30,* 457–501.

Manber, U. (1994). Finding similar files in a large file system. *Usenix Winter Technical Conference,* 1–10.

Marcus, G., & Davis, E. (2014, April 7). Eight (no, nine!) problems with big data. *The New York Times,* p. A23.

Marcus, M. P., Marcinkiewicz, M. A., & Santorini, B. (1993). Building a large annotated corpus of English: The Penn Treebank. *Computational Linguistics*, *19*(2), 313–330.

Maron, M. E., & Kuhns, J. L. (1960). On relevance, probabilistic indexing and information retrieval. *Journal of the Association of Computing Machinery*, *7*(3), 216–244.

Mason, Z. J. (2004). Cormet: A computational, corpus-based conventional metaphor extraction system. *Computational Linguistics*, *30*(1), 23–44.

Mathews, A. S. (2005). Power/knowledge, power/ignorance: Forest fires and the state in Mexico. *Human Ecology*, *33*(6), 795–820.

Mayer-Schönberger, V., & Cukier, K. (2013). *Big data: A revolution that will transform how we live, work, and think*. New York, NY: Houghton Mifflin Harcourt.

McCallum, A., & Li, W. (2003). Early results for named entity recognition with conditional random fields, feature induction and web-enhanced lexicons. In *Proceedings of the Seventh Conference on Natural Language Learning*. Stroudsburg, PA: Association for Computational Linguistics.

McCallum, A., & Nigam, K. (1998). *A comparison of event models for Naive Bayes text classification*. Paper presented at the AAAI-98 Workshop on Learning for Text Categorization. Retrieved from http://www.cs.cmu .edu/~knigam/papers/multinomial-aaaiws98.pdf

McKelvey, K. (2013). *Data science is engineering*. Retrieved June 27, 2015, from orgtheory.wordpress .com/2013/07/10/data-science-is-engineering-a-guest-post-by-karissa-mckelvey

Merton, R. K. (1968). *Social theory and social structure*. New York, NY: Free Press.

Metzler, D., Dumais, S. T., & Meek, C. (2007). Similarity measures for short segments of text. *ECIR '07 Proceedings of the Twenty-Ninth European Conference on IR Research* (pp. 16–27). Berlin, Germany: Springer-Verlag.

Mihalcea, R. (2007). Using Wikipedia for automatic word sense disambiguation. *Proceedings of NAACL HLT* (pp. 196–203). Stroudsburg, PA: Association for Computational Linguistics. Retrieved June 27, 2015, from aclweb.org/anthology/N07-1025

Mihalcea, R., Banea, C., & Wiebe, J. (2007). *Learning multilingual subjective language via cross-lingual projections*. Paper presented at the Proceedings of the Association for Computational Linguistics, Prague, Czech Republic.

Mihalcea, R., Corley, C., & Strapparava, C. (2006). Corpus-based and knowledge-based measures of text semantic similarity. pages 775–780. *AAAI '06 Proceedings of the Twenty-First Conference on Artificial intelligence—Volume 1* (pp. 775–780). Cambridge, MA: AAAI Press.

Mihalcea, R., & Pulman, S. (2009). Linguistic ethnography: Identifying dominant word classes in text. In A. Gelbukh (Ed.), *Computational linguistics and intelligent text processing* (pp. 594–602). Berlin, Heidelberg, Germany: Springer-Verlag Berlin Heidelberg.

Mihalcea, R., & Strapparava, C. (2009). The lie detector: Explorations in the automatic recognition of deceptive language. *Proceedings of the ACL-IJCNLP 2009 Conference Short Papers* (pp. 309–312). Stroudsburg, PA: Association for Computational Linguistics.

Mikolov, T., Yih, W.-T., & Zweig, G. (2013). *Linguistic regularities in continuous space word representations*. Paper presented at the Proceedings of the North American Chapter of the Association for Computational Linguistics: Human Language Technologies.

Miles, M. B., & Huberman, A. M. (1994). *Data management and analysis methods*. Thousand Oaks, CA: Sage.

Miller, G. A. (1995). WordNet: A lexical database for English. *Communications of the ACM*, *38*(11), 39–41.

Miller, G. A., & Charles, W. G. (1998). Contextual correlates of semantic similarity. *Language and Cognitive Processes*, *6*(1), 1–28.

Mische, A. (2014). Measuring futures in action: Projective grammars in the Rio+20 debates. *Theory & Society*, *43*(3–4), 437–464.

Mitchell, T., Russell, T., Broomhead, P., & Aldridge, N. (2002). Towards robust computerised marking of free-text responses. *Proceedings of the Sixth International Computer Assisted Assessment (CAA) Conference*. Leisestershire, England: Loughborough University.

Mohler, M., & Mihalcea, R. (2009). Text-to-text semantic similarity for automatic short answer grading. In *EACL '09 Proceedings of the Twelfth Conference of the European Chapter of the Association for Computational Linguistics* (pp. 567–575). Stroudsburg, PA: The Association for Computational Linguistics.

Mohr, J. W., & Bogdanov, P. (2013). Introduction—Topic models: What they are and why they matter. *Poetics*, *41*(6), 545–569.

Moser, K. (2000). Metaphor analysis in psychology—Method, theory, and fields of application. *Forum: Qualitative Social Research*, *1*(2) Art. 21.

Mukherjee, A., & Liu, B. (2012). Aspect extraction through semi-supervised modeling. In *Proceedings of the 50th Annual Meeting of the Association for Computational Linguistics*. Stroudsburg, PA: Association for Computational Linguistics.

Nadeau, D., & Sekine, S. (2007). A survey of named entity recognition and classification. *Lingvisticae Investigationes*, *30*(1), 3–26.

Nakagawa, T., Inui, K., & Kurohashi, S. (2010). Dependency tree-based sentiment classification using CRFs with hidden variables. In *Human Language Technologies: The 2010 Annual Conference of the North American Chapter of the Association for Computational Linguistics* (pp. 786–794). Stroudsburg, PA: Association for Computational Linguistics.

Neuman, Y., Assaf, D., Cohen, Y., Last, M., Argamon, S., Howard, N., & Frieder, O. (2013). Metaphor identification in large texts corpora. *PLoS One*, *8*(4).

Newman, M. L., Pennebaker, J. W., & Berry, D. S., & Richards, J. M. (2003). Lying words: Predicting deception from linguistic styles. *Personality and Social Psychology Bulletin*, *29*(5), 665–675.

Noel-Jorand, M. C., Reinert, M., Bonnon, M., & Therme, P. (1995). Discourse analysis and psychological adaptation to high altitude hypoxia. *Stress Medicine*, *11*(1), 27–39.

O'Halloran, K., & Coffin, C. (2004). Checking over-interpretation and under-interpretation: Help from corpora in critical linguistics. *Text and Texture: Systemic Functional Viewpoints on the Nature and Structure of Text*, 275–297.

O'Keefe, A., & Walsh, S. (2012). Applying corpus linguistics and conversation analysis in the investigation of small group teaching in higher education. *Corpus Linguistics and Linguistic Theory*, *8*(1), 159–181.

O'Neil, C., & Schutt, R. (2013). *Doing data science: Straight talk from the frontline*. Sebastopol, CA: O'Reilly Media.

Ortony, A., Clore, G. L., & Foss, M. A. (1987). The psychological foundations of the affective lexicon. *Journal of Personality and Social Psychology*, *53*, 751–766.

Ott, M., Choi, Y., Cardie, C., & Hancock, J. T. (2011). Finding deceptive opinion spam by any stretch of the imagination. *Proceedings of the Forty-Ninth Annual Meeting of the Association for Computational Linguistics: Human Language Technologies—Volume 1 Association for Computational Linguistics* (pp. 309–319) Stroudsburg, PA: Association for Computational Linguistics.

Page, L., Brin, S., Motwani, R., & Winograd, T. (1999). *The PageRank citation ranking: Bringing order to the web* (Technical report). Retrieved from Stanford University, Stanford InfoLab website: http://ilpubs.stanford .edu:8090/422

Pang, B., & Lee, L. (2004). A sentimental education: Sentiment analysis using subjectivity summarization based on minimum cuts. In *Proceedings of the Forty-Second Annual Meeting on Association for Computational Linguistics*. Stroudsburg, PA: Association for Computational Linguistics.

Pang, B., & Lee, L. (2008). Opinion mining and sentiment analysis. *Foundations and Trends in Information Retrieval*, *2*(1–2), 1–135.

Papineni, K. (2001). Why inverse document frequency? *Proceedings of the North American Chapter of the Association for Compuational*

Linguistics (NAACL) (pp. 25–32). Stroudsburg, PA: Association of Computational Lingusitics.

Papineni, K., Roukos, S., Ward, T., & Zhu, W.-J. (2002). Bleu: A method for automatic evaluation of machine translation. *Proceedings of the Fortieth Annual Meeting of the Association for Computational Linguistics* (pp. 311–318). Stroudsburg, PA: Association of Computational Linguistics.

Parker, I. (1992). *Discourse dynamics: Critical analysis for social and individual psychology*. London, England: Routledge.

Patton, M. Q. (1990). *Qualitative evaluation and research methods*. Newbury Park, CA: Sage.

Patton, M. Q. (2014). *Qualitative research & evaluation methods: Integrating theory and practice* (4th ed.). Thousand Oaks, CA: Sage.

Pauca, V. P., Shahnaz, F., Berry, M. W., & Plemmons, R. J. (2004). Text mining using non-negative matrix factorizations. *Proceedings of the Fourth SIAM International Conference on Data Mining*. Retrieved June 27, 2015, from epubs.siam.org/doi/ pdf/10.1137/1.9781611972740.45

Peirce, C. S. (1901). Truth and falsity and error. *Dictionary of Philosophy and Psychology*, *2*, 716–720.

Pennebaker, J. W., Francis, M., & Booth, R. J. (2001). *Linguistic Inquiry and Word Count (LIWC): A computerized text analysis program*. Mahwah, NJ: Lawrence Erlbaum.

Pennebaker, J. W., & King, L. (1999). Linguistic styles: Language use as an individual difference. *Journal of Personality and Social Psychology*, *77*, 1296–1312.

Pigliucci, M. (2009). The end of theory in science? *EMBO Reports*, *10*(6), 534.

Plummer, K. (1995). *Telling sexual stories: Power, change and social worlds.* London, England: Routledge.

Ponte, J. M., & Croft, W. B. (1998). A language modeling approach to information retrieval. In *SIGIR '98 Proceedings of the 21st Annual International ACM SIGIR Conference on Research and Development in Information Retrieval* (pp. 275–281). New York, NY: Association for Computing Machinery.

Popping, R. (1997). Computer programs for the analysis of texts and transcripts. In C. W. Roberts (Ed.), *Text analysis for the social sciences: Methods for drawing statistical inferences from texts and transcripts* (pp. 209–221). Mahwah, NJ: Lawrence Erlbaum.

Potter, J., & Wetherell, M. (1987). *Discourse and social psychology: Beyond attitudes and behavior.* Thousand Oaks, CA: Sage.

Propp, V. (1968). *Morphology of the folktale.* Austin: University of Texas Press.

Pulman, S. G., & Sukkarieh, J. Z. (2005). Automatic short answer marking. *EdAppsNLP 05 Proceedings of the Second Workshop on Building Educational Applications Using NLP* (pp. 9–16).

Qualitative Solutions and Research. (1997). *QSR NUD*IST 4: User Guide.* Thousand Oaks, CA: Sage.

Quinlan, J. (1993). *C4.5: Programs for machine learning.* San Francisco, CA: Morgan Kaufmann.

Quinn, K. M., Monroe, B. L., Colaresi, M., Crespin, M. H., & Radev, D. R. (2010). How to analyze political attention with minimal assumptions and costs. *American Journal of Political Science, 54*(1), 209–228.

Quinn, N. (1996). Culture and contradiction: The case of Americans reasoning about marriage. *Ethos, 24*(3), 391–425.

Quirk, R., Greenbaum, S., Leech, G., & Svartvik, J. (1985). *A comprehensive grammar of the English language.* New York, NY: Longman.

Reed, I. (2011). *Interpretation and social knowledge.* Chicago, IL: University of Chicago Press.

Rees, C. E., Knight, L. V., & Wilkinson, C. E. (2007). Doctors being up there and we being down here: A metaphorical analysis of talk about student/doctor-patient relationships. *Social Science and Medicine, 65*(4), 725–737.

Reinert, M. (1987). Un logiciel d'analyse des données textuelles: ALCESTE. Communication aux 5es Journées Internationales, Analyse de données et Informatique. Paris, France: INRIA.

Repko, A. F. (2012). *Interdisciplinary research: Process and theory.* Thousand Oaks, CA: Sage.

Resnik, P. (1995). Using information content to evaluate semantic similarity. In *IJCAI '95 Proceedings of the Fourteenth International Joint Conference on Artificial Intelligence* (pp. 448–453). San Francisco, CA: Morgan Kaufmann Publishers.

Resnik, P., Garron, A., & Resnik, R. (2013). Using topic modeling to improve prediction of neuroticism and depression in college students. In *Proceedings of the 2013 Conference on Empirical Methods in Natural Language Processing* (pp. 1348–1353). Stroudsburg, PA: Association for Computational Linguistics.

Richardson, D. C., Spivey, M. J., Barsalou, L. W., & McRae, K. (2003). Spatial representations activated during real-time comprehension of verbs. *Cognitive Science, 27*(5), 767–780.

Ricoeur, P. (1991). Narrative identity. *Philosophy Today, 35*(1), 73–81.

Riloff, E., & Jones, R. (1999). Learning dictionaries for information extraction by multi-level bootstrapping. In *Proceedings of the Sixteenth National Conference on Artificial Intelligence and the Eleventh Innovative Applications of Artificial Intelligence Conference Innovative Applications of Artificial Intelligence* (pp. 474–479). Menlo Park, CA: American Association for Artificial Intelligence.

Roberts, C. W. (Ed.). (1997). *Text analysis for the social sciences: Methods for drawing statistical inferences from texts and transcripts.* Mahwah, NJ: Lawrence Erlbaum.

Roberts, C. W. (2008). *The fifth modality: On languages that shape our motivations and cultures.* Leiden, Netherlands: Brill Publishers.

Roberts, C. W., Popping, R., & Pan, Y. (2009). Modalities of democratic transformation forms of public discourse in Hungary's largest newspaper, 1990–7. *International Sociology, 24*(4), 498–525.

Roberts, C. W., Zuell, C., Landmann, J., & Wang, Y. (2010). Modality analysis: A semantic grammar for imputations of intentionality in texts. *Quality & Quanity, 44*(2), 239–257.

Robertson, S. E., & Sparck Jones, K. (1976). Relevance weighting of search terms. *Journal of the American Society for Information Science, 27*(3), 129–146.

Rocchio, J. J. (1971). *Relevance feedback in information retrieval.* Englewood Cliffs, NJ: Prentice Hall.

Roderburg, S. (1998). *Sprachliche konstruktion der wirklichkeit. Metaphern in therapiegesprächen*. Wiesbaden, Germany: Deutscher Universitäts Verlag.

Roget, P. (1987). *Roget's thesaurus of English words and phrases*. New York, NY: Longman. (Original work published 1911)

Rojas, F. (2015). Computational sociology—From industry's side. Retrieved June 27, 2015, from orgtheory.wordpress.com/2015/01/05/computational-sociology-from-industrys-side

Rosenwald, G. C., & Ochberg, R. L. (1992). *Storied lives: The cultural politics of self-understanding*. New Haven, CT: Yale University Press.

Rousselière, D., & Vézina, M. (2009). Constructing the legitimacy of a financial cooperative in the cultural sector: A case study using textual analysis. *International Review of Sociology: Revue Internationale de Sociologie, 19*(2), 241–261.

Rubenstein, H., & Goodenough, J. B. (1965). Contextual correlates of synonymy. *Communications of the ACM, 8*(10), 627–633.

Ruiz Ruiz, J. (2009). Sociological discourse analysis: Methods and logic. *Forum: Qualitative Social Research, 10*(2). Retrieved June 27, 2015, from qualitative-research.net/index.php/fqs/article/view/1298/2882

Ryan, G. W., & Bernard, H. R. (2000). Data management and analysis methods. In N. K. Denzin & Y. S. Lincoln (Eds.), *Handbook of qualitative research* (2nd ed., pp. 769–802). Thousand Oaks, CA: Sage.

Ryan, G. W., & Bernard, H. R. (2003). Techniques to identify themes. *Field Methods, 15*(1), 85–109.

Ryan, G. W., & Bernard, H. R. (2010). *Analyzing qualitative data: Systematic approaches*. Thousand Oaks, CA: Sage.

Sahami, M., & Heilman, T. D. (2006). A web-based kernel function for measuring the similarity of short text snippets. In *WWW '06: Proceedings of the Fifteenth International Conference on World Wide Web* (pp. 377–386). New York, NY: Association for Computing Machinery.

Salmons, J. (2014). *Qualitative online interviews*. Thousand Oaks, CA: Sage.

Salton, G. (1989). *Automatic text processing: The transformation, analysis, and retrieval of information by computer*. Reading, PA: Addison-Wesley.

Salton, G., & Buckley, C. (1988). Term weighting approaches in automatic text retrieval. *Information Processing & Management, 24*(5), 513–523.

Salton, G., & Lesk, M. E. (1971). *The SMART retrieval system: Experiments in automatic document processing*. Upper Saddle River, NJ: Prentice Hall.

Salton, G., & McGill, M. (1986). *Introduction to modern information retrieval*. New York, NY: McGraw-Hill.

Salton, G., Singhal, A., Mitra, M., & Buckley, C. (1997). Automatic text structuring and summarization. *Information Processing and Management, 2*(32), 193–207.

Santa Ana, O. (2002). *Brown tide rising: Metaphors of Latinos in contemporary American public discourse*. Austin: University of Texas Press.

Saussure, de, F. (1959). *Course in general linguistics*. New York, NY: The Philosophical Library.

Schmidt, B. M. (2012). Words alone: Dismantling topic models in the humanities. *Journal of Digital Humanities, 2*(1).

Schmitt, R. (2000). Notes towards the analysis of metaphor. *Forum Qualitative Social Research, 1*(1).

Schmitt, R. (2005). Systematic metaphor analysis as a method of qualitative research. *The Qualitative Report, 10*(2), 358–394.

Schonhardt-Bailey, C. (2013). *Deliberating American monetary policy: A textual analysis*. Cambridge, MA: MIT Press.

Schradie, J. (2013). *Big data and the survival of the scientific method*. Retrieved May 31, 2015, from http://badhessian.org/2013/10/big-data-and-the-survival-of-the-scientific-method

Schuster, J., Beune, E., & Stronks, K. (2011). Metaphorical constructions of hypertension among three ethnic groups in the Netherlands. *Ethnicity and Health, 16*(6), 583–600.

Schutze, H. (1998). Automatic word sense discrimination. *Computational Linguistics, 24*(1), 97–124.

Shaw, J. (2014, March–April). Why "big data" is a big deal: Information science promises to change the world. *Harvard Magazine*. Retrieved June 27, 2015, from harvardmagazine.com/2014/03/why-big-data-is-a-big-deal

Shivakumar, N., & Garcia-Molina, H. (1995, June 11–13). Scam: A copy detection mechanism for digital documents. Paper presented at the Second International Conference in Theory and Practice of Digital Libraries, Austin, TX.

Silverman, D. (1993). *Interpreting qualitative data: Methods for analyzing talk, text and interaction*. Thousand Oaks, CA: Sage.

Silverman, D. (Ed.). (1997). *Qualitative research: Theory, method and practice.* Thousand Oaks, CA: Sage.

Smith, S., & Watson, J. (2010). *Reading autobiography: A guide for interpreting life narratives.* Minneapolis: University of Minnesota Press.

Snow, C. P. (1959). *The two cultures.* London, England: Cambridge University Press.

Socher, R., Perelygin, A., Wu, J. Y., Chuang, J., Manning, C. D., Ng, A. Y., & Potts, C. (2013). Recursive deep models for semantic compositionality over a sentiment treebank. In *Proceedings of the Conference on Empirical Methods in Natural Language Processing.* Retrieved from http://nlp.stanford.edu/~socherr/EMNLP2013_RNTN.pdf

Sparck Jones, K. (1972). A statistical interpretation of term specificity and its application in retrieval. *Journal of Documentation, 28*(1), 11–21.

Speed, G. J. (1893). Do newspapers now give the news? *Forum, 15,* 705–711.

Spradley, J. P. (1972). Adaptive strategies of urban nomads: The ethnoscience of tramp culture. In T. Weaver & D. J. White (Eds.), *The anthropology of urban environments.* Boulder, CO: Society for Applied Anthropology.

Stark, A., Shafran, I., & Kaye, J. (2012). Hello, who is calling?: Can words reveal the social nature of conversations? In *Proceedings of the 2012 Conference of the North American Chapters of the Association for Computational Linguistics: Human Language Technologies* (pp. 112–119).

Stone, P. J. (1968). *General inquirer: Computer approach to content analysis.* Cambridge, MA: MIT Press.

Stone, P. J., Dunphy, D. C., Smith, M. S., & Ogilvie, D. M. (1966). *The general inquirer: A computer approach to content analysis.* Cambridge, MA: MIT Press.

Stone, P. J., & Hunt, E. B. (1963). A computer approach to content analysis: Studies using the General Inquirer system. *AFIPS '63 (Spring) Proceedings of the May 21–23, 1963, Spring Joint Computer Conference* (pp. 241–256). doi:10.1145/1461551.1461583

Strapparava, C., & Mihalcea, R. (2007). Semeval-2007 task 14: Affective text. In *Proceedings of the Fourth International Workshop on the Semantic Evaluations,* Prague, Czech Republic (pp. 70–74). Stroudsburg, PA: Association for Computational Linguistics.

Strapparava, C., & Mihalcea, R. (2008). Learning to identify emotions in text. *SAC '08 Proceedings of the 2008 ACM Symposium on Applied Computing* (pp. 1556–1560).

Strapparava, C., & Valitutti, A. (2004, May). WordNet-Affect: An affective extension of WordNet. In *Proceedings of the Fourth International Conference on Language Resources and Evaluation* (pp. 1083–1086).

Strauss, C. (1992). What makes Tony run? Schemas as motives reconsidered. In R. D'Andrade & C. Strauss (Eds.), *Human motives and cultural models* (pp. 191–224). Cambridge, England: Cambridge University Press.

Strauss, C. (1997). Partly fragmented, partly integrated: An anthropological examination of "postmodern fragmented subjects." *Cultural Anthropology, 12*(3), 362–404.

Strauss, C., & Quinn, N. (1997). *A cognitive theory of cultural meaning.* Cambridge, England: Cambridge University Press.

Stubbs, M. (1994). Grammar, text, and ideology: Computer-assisted methods in the linguistics of representation. *Applied Linguistics, 15*(2), 210–223.

Sudhahar, S., Franzosi, R., & Cristianini, N. (2011). Automating quantitative narrative analysis of news data. *JMLR: Workshop and Conference Proceedings, 17,* 63–71.

Sudweeks, F., & Rafaeli, S. (1996). How do you get a hundred strangers to agree: Computer mediated communication and collaboration. In T. M. Harrison & T. D. Stephen (Eds.), *Computer networking and scholarship in the 21st century university* (pp. 115–136). New York, NY: SUNY Press.

Suerdem, A. K. (2010). Bridging qualitative and quantitative methods for classifying policy actors into policy discourse communities: Thematic analysis and formal concept analysis approaches. *International Journal of Data Analysis Techniques and Strategies, 2*(3). doi:10.1504/IJDATS.2010.034056

Sveningsson, M. (2003). Ethics in Internet ethnography. *International Journal of Global Information Management, 11*(3), 45–60.

Sweetser, E. (1990). *From etymology to pragmatics: The mind-body metaphor in semantic structure and semantic change.* Cambridge, England: Cambridge University Press.

Takamura, H., Inui, T., & Okumura, M. (2006). Latent variable models for semantic orientations of phrases. In *Proceedings of the Eleventh Meeting of the European Chapter of the Association for Computational Linguistics* (pp. 201–208). Trento, Italy.

Toerien, M., & Wilkinson, S. (2004). Exploring the depilation norm: A qualitative questionnaire study of women's body hair removal. *Qualitative Research in Psychology, 1*(1), 69–92.

Trochim, W. M. K. (1989). Concept mapping: Soft science or hard art? *Science Direct, 12*(1), 87–110. doi:10.1016/0149-7189(89)90027-X

Trochim, W. M. K., Cook, J. A., & Setze, R. (1994). Using concept mapping to develop a conceptual framework of staff's views of a supported employment program for individuals with severe mental illness. *Journal of Consulting and Clinical Psychology, 62*(4), 766–775.

Turney, P. D. (2001). Mining the web for synonyms: PMI-IR versus LSA on TOEFL. In L. De Raedt & P. Flach (Eds.), *Lecture Notes in Computer Science: Vol. 2167. Machine Learning: ECML 2001* (pp. 491–502).

Turney, P. D. (2002). Thumbs up or thumbs down? semantic orientation applied to unsupervised classification of reviews. In *Proceedings of the Fortieth Annual Meeting on Association for Computational Linguistics* (pp. 417–424). Stroudsburg, PA: Association for Computational Linguistics.

Turney, P. D., Neuman, Y., Assaf, D., & Cohen, Y. (2011). Literal and metaphorical sense identification through concrete and abstract context. In *EMNLP '11 Proceedings of the Conference on Empirical Methods in Natural Language Processing*, (pp. 680–690). Stroudsburg, PA: Association for Computational Linguistics.

van Dijk, T. A. (1993). Principles of critical discourse analysis. *Discourse & Society, 4*(2), 249–283.

van Ham, F., Wattenberg, M., & Viégas, F. B. (2009). Mapping text with phrase nets. *Visualization and Computer Graphics, 15*(6), 1169–1176.

Van Herzele, A. (2006). A forest for each city and town: Story lines in the policy debate for urban forests in Flanders. *Urban Studies, 43*(3), 673–696. doi:10.1080/00420980500534651

van Meter, K. M., & Saint Léger, M. de. (2014). American, French & German sociologies compared through link analysis of conference abstracts. *Bulletin of Sociological Methodology, 122*(1), 26–45.

Vapnik, V. (1995). *The nature of statistical learning theory*. New York, NY: Springer.

Viégas, F. B., & Wattenberg, M. (2008). TIMELINES: Tag clouds and the case for vernacular visualization. *Interactions, 15*(4), 49–52. doi:10.1145/1374489.1374501

Walejko, G. (2009). Online survey: Instant publication, instant mistake, all of the above. In E. Hargittai (Ed.), *Research confidential: Solutions to problems most social scientists pretend they never have* (pp. 101–115). Ann Arbor: University of Michigan Press.

Wattenberg, M., & Viégas, F. B. (2008). The word tree, and interactive visual concordance. *Visualization and Computer Graphics, 14*(6), 1221–1228.

Weale, A., Bicquelet, A., & Bara, L. (2012). Debating abortion, deliberative reciprocity and parliamentary advocacy. *Political Studies, 60*(3), 643–667.

Weisgerber, C., & Butler, S. H. (2009). Visualizing the future of interaction studies: Data visualization applications as a research, pedagogical, and presentational tool for interaction scholars. *The Electronic Journal of Communication, 19*(1–2). Retrieved from http://www.cios.org/ejcpublic/019/1/019125.HTML

Wertsch, J. V. (1985). *Vygotsky and the social formation of mind*. Cambridge, MA: Harvard University Press.

Wetherell, M., & Edley, N. (1999). Negotiating hegemonic masculinity: Imaginary positions and psycho-discursive practices. *Feminism and Psychology, 9*(3), 335–356.

Wheeldon, J., & Ahlberg, M. K. (2012). *Visualizing social science research: Maps, methods, & meaning*. Thousand Oaks, CA: Sage.

Wheeldon, J., & Faubert, J. (2009). Framing experience: Concept maps, mind maps, and data collection in qualitative research. *International Journal of Qualitative Methods, 83*(3), 68–83.

White, H. (1978). *Tropics of discourse: Essays in cultural criticism*. Baltimore, MD: The Johns Hopkins University Press.

White, M. J., Judd, M. D., & Poliandri, S. (2012). Illumination with a dim bulb? What do social scientists learn by employing qualitative data analysis software in the service of multimethod designs? *Sociological Methodology, 42*(1), 43–76.

White, P. W. (1924). Quarter century survey of press content shows demand for facts. *Editor and Publisher, 57*.

Wiebe, J., Bruce, R., & O'Hara, T. (1999). Development and use of a gold-standard data set for subjectivity classifications. In *Proceedings of the Thirty-Seventh Annual Meeting of the Association for Computational Linguistics* (pp. 246–253). Stroudsburg, PA: Association for Computational Linguistics.

Wiebe, J., & Mihalcea, R. (2006). *Word sense and subjectivity*. Paper presented at the Forty-Fourth Annual Meeting of the Association for Computational Linguistics, Sydney, Australia.

Wiebe, J., Wilson, T., & Cardie, C. (2005). Annotating expressions of opinions and emotions in language. *Language Resources and Evaluation, 39*(2–3), 165–210.

Wilcox, D. F. (1900). The American newspaper: A study in social psychology. *The ANNALS of the American Academy of Political and Social Science, 16*(1), 56–92. doi:10.1177/000271620001600104

Wilkinson, L., & Friendly, M. (2009). The history of the cluster heat map. *The American Statiscian, 63*(9), 179–184. doi:10.1198/tas.2009).0033

Wilson, T. (2008). *Fine-grained subjectivity and sentiment analysis: Recognizing the intensity, polarity, and attitudes of private states* (PhD thesis). University of Pittsburgh, Pennsylvania.

Winkel, G. (2012). Foucault in the forests—A review of the use of "Foucauldian" concepts in forest policy analysis. *Forest Policy and Economics, 16*, 81–92.

Woodwell, D. (2014). *Research foundations: How do we know what we know?* Thousand Oaks, CA: Sage.

Wu, Z., & Palmer, M. (1994). Verb semantics and lexical selection. In J. Pustejovsky (Ed.), *ACL '94 Proceedings of the Thirty-Second Annual Meeting on Association for Computational Linguistics* (pp. 133–138). Stroudsburg, PA: Association for Computational Linguistics.

Yarowsky, D. (1995). Unsupervised word sense disambiguation rivaling supervised methods. In *Proceedings of the Thirty-Third Annual Meeting on Association for Computational Linguistics*. Stroudsburg, PA: Association for Computational Linguistics.

Yih, W.-T., & Meek, C. (2007). Improving similarity measures for short segments of text. In A. Cohn (Ed.), *AAAI '07: Proceedings of the Twenty-Second National Conference on Artificial Intelligence*—Volume 2 (pp. 1489–1494). Cambridge, MA: AAAI Press.

Yu, H., & Hatzivassiloglou, V. (2003). Towards answering opinion questions: Separating facts from opinions and identifying the polarity of opinion sentences. Paper presented at the Conference on Empirical Methods in Natural Language Processing, Sapporo, Japan.

Yun, G. W., & Trumbo, C. W. (2000). Comparative response to a survey executed by post, e-mail, & web form. *Journal of Computer-Mediated Communication, 6*(1).

Zagibalov, T., & Carroll, J. (2008). Automatic seed word selection for unsupervised sentiment classification of Chinese text. In *Proceedings of the Twenty-Second International Conference on Computational Linguistics* (pp. 1073–1080). Stroudsburg, PA: Association for Computational Linguistics.

Zhou, L. (2014, June 7). Facebook plans event to recruit sociologists. *VentureBeat*. Retrieved from http://venturebeat.com/2014/06/07/exclusive-to-sell-ads-in-the-developing-world-facebook-is-hiring-sociologists

• Index •